Army Brat,
Army Bride,
Civilian: *A Life*

Army Brat, Army Bride, Civilian: *A Life*

DARLENE GRAVETT

an imprint of The Reader's Digest Association, Inc.

LifeRich Publishing books may be ordered through booksellers or by contacting:

LifeRich Publishing
1663 Liberty Drive
Bloomington, IN 47403
www.liferichpublishing.com
1 (888) 238-8637

ISBN: 978-1-4897-0065-0 (e)
ISBN: 978-1-4897-0064-3 (sc)

Printed in the United States of America.

LifeRich Publishing rev. date: 11/15/2013

*This book is dedicated to
the memory of my parents,
Arthur Whitfield Johnson and
Nadine Mae Smith Johnson,
and to the memory of my sister,
Rachel Marie Johnson Gomilla*

CONTENTS

PART 3   CIVILIAN

PREFACE

In Mary Edwards Wertsch's groundbreaking book on growing up as a military brat, *Military Brats: Legacies of Childhood Inside the Fortress,* she writes in her preface that after seeing the movie *The Great Santini,* based on Pat Conroy's book, she began thinking about the differences between her life and that of civilians. She writes, "They came from real places. I didn't. They knew their relatives. I didn't. They identified with a region of the country. I didn't." I discovered this book as I began thinking of writing about my own life and my lack of roots. I can identify with Mary and with so many of the military brats that she interviewed and quoted in the book.

Pat Conroy wrote the introduction to the book, and it also spoke to me. He writes, "I think being a military brat is one of the strangest and most interesting ways to spend an American childhood. The military brats of America are an invisible, unorganized tribe, a federation of brothers and sisters bound by common experience, by our uniformed fathers [and mothers], by the movement of families being rotated through the American mainland and to military posts in foreign lands. We are an undiscovered nation living invisibly in the body politic of this country. There are millions of us scattered throughout America, but we have no special markings or passwords to identify each other when we move into a common field of vision. We grew up strangers to ourselves. We passed through our military childhoods unremembered. We were transients, billboards to be changed, body temperatures occupying school desks for a short time."

These words resonate with me because I too was a military brat—specifically, an Army one, and have never felt truly "at home" anywhere. I was also a military wife, so I continued the transitory existence with which I was already familiar when I married. This is my story of the difficulties and joys that can come with that kind of life.

"Be true to yourself and to the culture you were born into,
. . . . Tell your story as only you can tell it."
William Zinsser

INTRODUCTION

Usually one of the first questions people ask each other upon meeting for the first time is "Where are you from?" For years I had no idea how to answer that question. I might say I was born in Roanoke, VA. However, I had left there at the age of ten and had been back only to visit relatives, other than spending part of one miserable year there as a junior in high school, so I never really felt that Roanoke was home and still don't. Basically, my home was where I lived at the time. Mary Edwards Wertsch covers this dilemma well in her book *Military Brats: Legacies of Childhood Inside the Fortress.* She writes, "There are two questions one can pose that reveal rootlessness as instantly as a litmus test. The first: *Where are you from?* The second . . . *Where do you want to be buried?*" (249-50) I still have problems with the first question even though I now answer it the same way every time, and I am beginning to think about the second, for which I do not have an answer.

As a former "Army brat" who became an Army bride, I have lived in more than thirty-five different homes—sometimes in foreign countries, other times in various states. Often, I have moved two or three times to different houses or apartments within the same city or town or from one of those to quarters on an Army post as a set became available. Army quarters range from multi-family apartments to duplexes to large houses, depending on one's rank and availability of housing, and most military folks get to sample a little bit of everything during their careers.

My first identification of myself is as an "Army brat," but not the annoying kind of brat, which places a negative value on the word--although I can attest to the fact that I could be bratty at times, and my mother called us three kids brats more than once. Instead, in military lingo the word normally has a positive spin and means simply the child of a career military person that has traveled, seen, and experienced much. Most of us former military brats are proud to have that label because to us the term means we were part of a subculture of kids who moved frequently, adjusted quickly, and learned resilience.

During what I call the second phase of my life, I became an Army bride by marrying a second lieutenant in the Army and continuing to move frequently, though not so often as my family had moved when I was a child. Being married to Ray meant that the standard of living was much improved, and the military quarters were considerably better because of the difference between my father's status as a non-commissioned officer and my husband's as an officer. It was still military living, though, which required the flexibility and survival skills that I had learned earlier in life.

The third stage of my life is the civilian one, during which I have actually lived in the same house for twenty plus years and have been able to become actively involved in the community. Before we moved into our current house in North Carolina, we had lived in the same house in South Carolina for ten years—our first civilian experience after retirement from the Army. Thus, for the last thirty plus years I have been able to establish roots and have a possible answer to the question "Where are you from?"

In writing this book, I have looked back over my life both as an Army brat as well as an Army bride and have been as honest as possible in showing both the good and the bad. Military life is not for everyone. I saw more than one spouse have to go back home from an overseas post because she (spouses were mostly women in the fifties and sixties) simply could not adjust. Military life instills loyalty and patriotism, not only in the one who is actually serving but also in the whole family. To this day I do not like seeing people ignore our national anthem when it is played at ballgames and other attractions. I find that there is almost a feeling of apathy and nonchalance on the part of many. I am not sure some folks know what they should do when the national anthem is played. Even more upsetting is the fact that many people, both old and young, do not seem to know the words to this patriotic song.

My hope in writing this book is that it will help those who have not grown up in the military understand and maybe gain an appreciation for that life, including the sacrifices and constant upheavals that go along with it. I realize that, in spite of the problems military families encountered during the Vietnam War, the sacrifices have been many times more difficult for those who have been involved with the wars in Iraq and Afghanistan because of the frequent reassignments to those places. Being in the military during times of war is, of course, the hardest of all; however, living the military life during "normal" times has its challenges as well.

PART ONE
ARMY BRAT

Darlene, Age 6

CHAPTER ONE

So Many Moves, So Many Schools

"Here are the movers, Mother." It was January 1959, and I was at home in Elizabethtown, KY, waiting for the men to come and pack up my meager belongings to take to Lawton, Oklahoma, so that I could join my husband of about a month, who was already at his first duty station, Fort Sill. I owned very little, as I had just completed the first semester of my senior year of college and had always lived either at home or in a campus dorm room. There were clothes, a couple of trunks, and a few linens and kitchen items I had received at my bridal shower. It took less than two hours to pack it all up and put it into a small moving van.

Mother had made sure to tell the movers that when our family had moved around in the Army, there had been so much more furniture and that it would take almost a whole day to pack her stuff. What I knew was that we actually had not had much at all since everything we owned fit into a 950-square foot house, but bragging like that helped my mother feel better about herself.

Like other military families, we had moved from one Army post to another, which had meant for me from one school to another, often in a different state or country, usually settling into a small rental apartment or house because that's all we could afford, and until Daddy got to be a sergeant, Army quarters were not available. One time, with my mother's help, I counted twenty addresses we had had from my birth to being a senior in high school. Sometimes we lived in a place only a few months, especially during Daddy's civilian phase. Before he went into the Army, he had worked at various jobs—driving a truck, selling produce, moving furniture, working at a gas station—in Roanoke, VA, where I was born in 1937.

My parents had married in 1935; he was 19, she was 20. Daddy had enlisted in the Army, only to leave after a few years but then go back in because at least the Army provided a steady paycheck, and the 1930s were tough times for lots of families. It was not unusual to eat mayonnaise sandwiches for lunch and beans, potatoes, and cornbread for supper. As a child, I remember hating the fact that I was never anywhere long enough to make friends or get established as a good student in school. As a result, I was a shy child, unsure of myself and afraid to express any opinion I might have. Actually, I probably had very few opinions. At home the prevailing attitude was that children were to be seen and not heard, stated often by my parents as well as Grandmother Johnson, my dad's mother.

A particularly traumatic time was when Daddy went overseas during World War II. I was about seven years old and my brother, four. My mother had a difficult time parenting by herself, and I remember writing a secret letter to my dad complaining about the way Mother was behaving—being too friendly with the man who delivered our heating oil, for example, and being what I thought was mean to us, such as washing our faces at night with a cold wash cloth to keep us awake longer because she thought that would make us sleep later in the morning. Unfortunately, my dad wrote back to my mother and told her what I had written and asked her what was going on. Of course, Mother was furious with me, but she made sure that she behaved herself when we kids were around from then on.

My brother and I were close enough in age to have the usual brother-sister conflicts, but we generally got along okay. However, because I was nine years old by the time my sister, Rachel, was born, I thought she was something that my parents had done to punish me. I could not figure out why my brother and I were not enough of a family without this other one. I had been able to tattle on my brother and keep him in trouble almost constantly; this cuddly new thing was a different matter. She received far too much attention to suit me. As she grew older, the situation became much worse. I was actually expected to take her with me when I went swimming or elsewhere with my friends and, at times, was a built-in babysitter with no pay. I thought the whole matter was an injustice and, as a result, my sister and I did not become friends until much later in life after we were both married and living in different states.

Growing up, my sister and I had had to share a bedroom while my brother, since he was the only boy, always got to have his own room. This was another injustice and an infringement on my freedom. Years later my sister told me how happy she was the day I left for college because she finally had the whole room to herself, such as it was, probably no larger than ten by ten. The feeling was mutual because I was ecstatic to be leaving home and be on my own.

Since we moved so often, I attended lots of different elementary schools in Roanoke. I was always a good, obedient, hardworking student, in spite of oftentimes coming into a class in the middle of the year. I still remember clearly the incident that happened to me when I was in the 4th grade. We had moved to another school district in the fall of the year. I always liked to sit near the front of the room, but all of the seats in and near the front were taken by the time I entered, so Mrs. Brown, the teacher, placed me in the very last seat on one of the rows. I hated being back there because it made my feeling of isolation worse than it already was. Christmas was approaching, and Mrs. Brown told us in class one day, "On Monday bring a gift for one of your classmates, and we will exchange gifts."

I had not made any friends in the class yet, but I had Mother pick me up something for Mary, the most popular girl in the class, who, of course, sat in one of the front seats. I did have a friend, but she was in another class. When the time came to exchange gifts, everyone in the class received a gift but me. I was deeply hurt and embarrassed at how obvious it was that no one had cared enough to bring me anything. But to make matters much worse, Mary turned around and noticed I had nothing, so in her attempt to be nice, she shouted at me from her spot in front all the way to the back row, "I brought you something, Darlene, but I lost it on the way to school."

After that, anyone who had not noticed that I had no gift now realized it, and my mortification was so great, it was all I could do to get through the day. I cried all the way home and continued crying into the night. Mother tried to soothe my wounded feelings as best she could. I often related this story to my first-year English classes when I asked them to write of an experience they had never forgotten. I have also often wondered if Mrs. Brown, who was pregnant at the time, learned from that experience to either draw names or have a gift or two put aside in case some child does not receive something. I cannot remember the names of any of my other elementary school teachers, but I will never forget Mrs. Brown's name because of this incident.

It was always very important to try to fit in wherever I happened to be; I did not want to feel like an outsider, but usually I did, at least for the first few weeks until I could make friends. I remember at one elementary school in Roanoke I discovered I was not making my "r's" the way all of the other kids were. So I practiced and practiced my cursive until I could write an "r" the way they did. I still write my "r's" that way—close to a "v" and now it is the old-fashioned way to write that letter, and most people under sixty have a difficult time reading it!

On December 6, 1947, in the middle of the 5th grade for me and the 1st grade for my brother, Richard, we sailed to the Panama Canal Zone to be with our dad, who had received military orders to go there and had left several months before. It was not uncommon for the member of the military to go on ahead of the family until quarters became available at the new duty station. This journey was quite an arduous one for Mother, who had a difficult time dealing with the three of us. I was ten years old at the time, Richard was seven, and Rachel was eighteen months. Back in those days the military used ships to get families to and from most overseas destinations.

I can remember Richard and me having a wonderful time on the ship. We played everywhere we could, ran away from Mother and hid, listened to one of the crew members tell stories to us, and basically were hard to control, especially since Mother had to stay close to the baby. After a trip of nine days, including a stop of seventy-two hours during which the ship was docked at Puerto Rico and we got to sightsee, Daddy met us and took us to a big set of Army quarters. The main thing I remember was when he opened a closet door and exclaimed: "Look what a surprise I have for you!" The surprise was a huge stalk of bananas hanging from the rod in the closet! We thought we had died and gone to heaven; we had never seen so many bananas, and I guess we did not realize that that is how they grew!

Our four and a half years in the Panama Canal Zone, first at Fort Sherman on the Atlantic side for about eight months and then at Fort Clayton on the Pacific side, were probably the best years our family had. We certainly lived there longer than anywhere else during my growing up years. Daddy took on an additional job as a theatre manager at the Fort Clayton theatre, which brought him extra money and allowed us to get into the movies free.

I learned to swim on post in an Olympic-size swimming pool. We would rent a cabin and spend weekends at Santa Clara Beach. We lived in a lovely three-bedroom duplex on a cul-de-sac, where my brother and I, along with the other neighborhood kids, played kickball in front of our quarters. Except for the normal growing pains of becoming a teenager, it was a wonderful, carefree existence. Even my parents seemed to get along better, probably because they were away from the relatives, and they had enough money to enjoy life for a change. I had always wanted to take piano lessons, so they bought me a used piano and I had about 18 months of lessons before we had to move; that was the only piano we ever had and my last piano lessons.

When I got into the 6th grade, I was thrilled to stay at the same school—Balboa Junior High School—for three wonderful years and then go on to the 9th grade at Balboa High School with the same kids attending that I had known in junior high. I was beginning to feel almost normal and had begun to realize that I had the brains to do something with my life. In truth, I had always thought of myself as being special because I have a visible birthmark on my forehead, and I saw that as a symbol that I was indeed marked to be somebody or do something important some day! (How egocentric we can be at a young age.)

We left the Panama Canal Zone on June 15, 1952, before I was to begin my sophomore year. My dad was reassigned to Fort Hood, Texas, and the Army actually flew us back instead of having us go by ship. We landed in New Orleans, drove to Roanoke, VA, to visit family for a few days, and then drove to Texas. We moved into an Army area called Hood Village; the housing was just about what it sounded like. The World War II buildings were long, one-story, tar paper-covered structures consisting of small apartments. Because our family was considered large, we were given two apartments with the wall separating them taken down, yet two kitchens remained. The space was adequate, but it was still a shabby place to have to live, and I am sure it was the reason my folks made the decision to buy a house a few months later.

I attended 10th grade at Fort Hood High School, which was quite small and required an adjustment after having attended a large high school the previous year. Since I had completed Algebra I at Balboa High School during my freshman year, I signed up for geometry, as that seemed to be the next logical sequence and what was recommended for me to take. When the semester started, I saw that there were only six of us in the geometry class—five boys and me. I thought it was a little strange, but I figured I would just have to live with it. After the bell rang at the end of the class, the male teacher asked me to stay. I will never forget his words: "Darlene, you are welcome to remain in the class, but it might be a little difficult for you at times to put up with the antics of the boys."

I got the distinct impression that he felt uncomfortable with me in there and would rather I take another course, although he did not say that. In today's world this teacher would be sued, or the parents would get involved! My parents did not know enough about the different classes to do anything but fuss about it. They would not have dreamed of going to the school and talking with the principal. Being the shy girl I was and not knowing anyone to discuss the matter with—no school counselors in those days and I had yet to make friends--I was upset but not assertive enough to stay in the class. Thus, I had to switch to Algebra II, a class I hated and never did understand, even though I made A's all year in it! I never took another advanced math course after that, not even in college. I have often wondered what would have happened if I had stayed in the class and suffered through it. Maybe my attitude toward math would be better.

It was during my sophomore year at Fort Hood that I had a wonderful English teacher, Mrs. Ballard, who served as a role model for me in the way she organized her classes and the way she taught. I wanted to be an English teacher just like her, and once this idea took hold of me, it never let go. I loved my English classes and had always made mostly A's in them once I got into high school, even with all the moves. Good grades in English did not translate into cash, however, and since money was always tight around our house, I needed to find a part-time job.

Being new to the area, I did not know anyone who owned a business or who was in a position to put in a good word for me. So I simply gathered up my courage and went into the nearby town, Killeen, and asked for a job. I was hired to work in what was then called a "dime store." Unfortunately, my first attempt at holding a job did not go well. I was put to work at the candy counter with an experienced girl showing me the ropes. In addition to teaching me how to weigh and charge for the candy and how to use the cash register, she also showed me how to snitch a piece of candy, all the time assuring me that it was fine, the boss did not mind. Apparently, the boss did mind, for I was let go at the end of the day. I was crushed and realized immediately what an idiot I had been. My conscience bothered me, but I had learned a valuable lesson.

I decided to try the other dime store in town, but I was so afraid that the manager from the first place had already clued in the manager of the second place about what a bad employee I was. (Again, how the world revolves around us when we are young!) Surprisingly, I did get a job right away at the second store, this time in the hardware department, about which I knew nothing. However, I learned to make keys and became a model employee. Of course, I was not there too long before our family moved, and I would not try for another job until I was a senior in high school.

CHAPTER TWO

My Junior Year, Two High Schools

Even though it happened in December 1953, I will never forget the details of my junior year in high school. Mother and Daddy had bought a house in the spring of my sophomore year—the first house we had ever owned. We all enjoyed a nice new house after having lived in Hood Village. We had been living in it for only a few months when Daddy received military orders for Germany. At first, we three kids were excited, until we discovered that we would not be going with him. Instead, he would have to go on ahead of us, and we would wait for our port call before we could join him. The port call was an official letter giving the date we would embark, the name of the ship, and the specific location.

As usual, Mother saw the situation as another burden that had been placed upon her. Back then most women generally did not deal with the family's financial matters or the details associated with selling a house—particularly not Mother, who had little confidence in herself. Therefore, she insisted that my dad sell the house before he left. The rest of her plan was that we (she and the three of us) would go to Salem, Virginia, to stay with Grandma Johnson and wait on the port call. Since we would be sailing from New York, it made perfect sense to Mother for us to be in Virginia rather than way out in Texas when the port call came, in spite of the facts that Mother and Grandmother Johnson had never gotten along very well and it would mean that we three kids would be attending three different schools in the same year.

So we followed her plan. After about the first six weeks of school, during which I attended my third high school--the new, consolidated, large Fort Hood/Killeen High School, the house was sold, and Daddy was in Germany. Mother and the three of us took the train, a common mode of travel in the 50s, from Killeen to Roanoke, Virginia. We were picked up by my Uncle Royce, Daddy's brother-in-law, and driven to the town of Salem, where we settled into Grandma Johnson's small house to await our port call, under the assumption that it would be only a matter of weeks. We had brought with us just our suitcases holding the clothes we would need for a couple of months. Our furniture and personal belongings had already been sent on to Germany.

There was more to Mother's plan, however, than simply that part. She wanted me to attend the same high school that she had attended, which meant leaving Salem on a bus every Sunday afternoon, going to my great-aunt's upstairs apartment in Roanoke, living with her during the week while attending Jefferson High School in downtown

Roanoke, and then taking the bus back to my grandma's house on Friday afternoons. We had no car, but Mother did not know how to drive at that time anyway. My great aunt, called "Aint" Eddie, already had her older sister, Pearl, living with her, and, since it was only a two-bedroom apartment, I slept on a cot in Aint Eddie's bedroom.

Of all my relatives Aint Eddie was by far the most eccentric. She had been married twice but never had children of her own; however, she would take in various family members as they needed a place to stay. Visiting her over the years was always a special event because she would cook up piles of food, such as frying a whole pound of bacon and a dozen eggs for breakfast for two people! In her later years she made wine--tomato, strawberry, elderberry, and different kinds of grape, keeping it in jars under the guest bed on her screened-in porch. While she would offer her guests the wine, she preferred sipping on beer during the day herself. She worked until her retirement in the linen room of Lewis-Gale Hospital in Roanoke, VA, but never made over $210 a week. She lived to be 94 years old.

My year with her was very difficult. By coming into the school a couple of months after everyone else had started, I did not know a soul in the entire high school, which, of course, was not unusual. However, as a teenager having to live with two elderly women who didn't know a thing about life in a modern high school or even contemporary music was difficult. I remember bringing a girl friend back to the apartment one day after school to visit, and when Aint Eddie got home from work, she came into the bedroom where we were doing homework and talking and told us to roll back the rug and dance; she put on the record "Wabash Cannonball" to help us out. That song was an antique even then, and the incident was quite an embarrassment to me. I never brought anyone else to the apartment. I loved my great-aunt and appreciated her hospitality, but my living arrangement made me even more of an outsider. I truly felt as though I did not have a home the entire year.

Jefferson High was a very large high school; I had come from a small one. I had a difficult time making friends, usually ate alone in the lunch room, and found myself totally miserable. I had no social life; in fact, I did not have a date with a boy the entire year. It did not help that the curricula were not exactly alike: I had been enrolled in a speech class in Texas; here I had to take play production. For a shy 16-year-old who knew no one and had trouble standing in front of a class, I was embarrassed more than once. I just kept thinking to myself, "This will be over as soon as our port call arrives and we can head to Germany."

We had been expecting our port call just any day. As December approached, Mother had been given assurances by my dad in his letters that the port call would come before Christmas. Therefore, she decided that the best thing to do would be for us kids to check out of our schools before the Christmas break because we surely would not be going back. I gleefully told my teachers and the two girls that I was beginning to be friends with good-bye and went back to Salem, ready to go to Germany.

Then the unthinkable happened. On the same day in December that Mother received the long-awaited port call, giving her the day and time our ship would sail, she also received a telegram from my father saying that he was ill and was returning to the States. Chaos set in. Mother's emotions ranged from anger to hysterical crying and back again. Taking our cues from her dramatic reaction, the three of us wailed: "What are we going to do? Where will we go now? What will become of us? What about school?"

Daddy returned and the answers became clear. We had to stay where we were and finish out our school year. Richard and Rachel had been attending an elementary school in Salem, a couple of blocks from Grandma's house, so it was a lot easier for them. In fact, Richard looks back on this year as a fun one. For me, as a self-conscious teenager, to have to return to that large high school after having proudly told the teachers and my classmates that I was leaving to live in Germany was almost too much to bear. Not only was my pride hurt, I felt as though my whole life had been ruined. How was I going to face everybody at school?

However, after Christmas I did what I had to do: I went back and continued my weekly routine for the rest of the school year. Thus, my junior year was by far the worst year of my life, for I felt that I really did not quite fit in anywhere—not in Grandma's small house, not in Aint Eddie's upstairs apartment, nor at Jefferson High School. I was thrilled when my dad, who had been reassigned to Fort Knox, KY, came to get us at the end of the school year so that we could join him in Elizabethtown, and I could have a fresh start in a new school in another state, for I knew the next year had to be better than the last, even though it would be the fifth high school I had attended, beginning with my freshman year at Balboa High in the Panama Canal Zone.

As I look back over that year, I realize that I gave little thought to the effect all of these events had on my Grandma Johnson. It must have been quite trying for her to have our family living with her in that small house all of those months. She was working at a hospital as a nurse's aide on the evening shift, which meant she had to sleep during the day. I do remember some bitter arguments taking place between her and Mother, and I even had a spat with Grandma myself. Our tempers must have been really short; it was a very difficult time for all of us. However, I now realize that even though my folks did not make the wisest decisions, causing the family to suffer in many ways, they did what they thought was best at the time. And what I went through that year did not permanently damage me, but instead helped me have a successful, fulfilling year as a senior and also probably contributed to my ability to adapt to the various roles I have had to play in my adult life.

My senior year of high school was a very rewarding experience; I attended Elizabethtown High School for the entire year with only one move from a two-bedroom rental house to our own three-bedroom home in the same housing area. It was small for a family of five—not even a thousand square feet and only one small bathroom, so tiny that I broke my little toe one day trying to do a cheerleading jump in it. (I was never a cheerleader; I was simply trying to emulate one.) Of course, having only one bathroom was not unusual for the 50s. It was comforting to be back in a smaller community and a much smaller high school; there were only forty-seven students in my class, and I graduated fifth highest. Considering how much I had moved during my high school years, I was proud of that achievement.

As usual, not long after we moved to Elizabethtown, or E'Town as it was and is known, I realized that I desperately needed a job in order to earn some money to buy things my family could not afford to give me. Again, I lucked out and got the first job I applied for. My family and I had stopped at a barbecue restaurant between Elizabethtown and Fort Knox, and I noticed a Help Wanted sign in the window. I commented on it, and Daddy said, "Why don't you go in and see about it?" I did and was hired immediately. The only problem was that the restaurant was several miles from where we lived, and I did not drive yet. I would learn that year, but we had only one car which Daddy took to work. My mother still did not drive, but she would learn within a few years--after I graduated from college.

While I was working at the restaurant on weekends, I had to figure out every day how I would get to work and back, which was a pain. I somehow managed, thanks to the owners, who lived in my neighborhood. I really enjoyed my work as a waitress; it was good exercise, the restaurant did a great business, and the tips were nice to have.

One memory that stands out from my senior year was the time my brother came to my rescue. In order to raise money for our senior trip, we students decided to sell magazine subscriptions door to door. I went to each house asking my neighbors to buy at least one magazine subscription, but I had to return home a couple of hours later without having sold even one! I was so dejected that Richard volunteered to try selling them. An hour later he was back and had sold several subscriptions; he had gone to the same houses that I had! I saw right then that he was the salesman in the family; he would go on to become an outstanding salesman for Kentucky Pen Company and later the successful owner of more than one Xerox store. I definitely was not good at sales, a fact which only confirmed my goal of becoming a teacher.

Even though Elizabethtown High School mainly had civilian students, they were familiar with the military, as Fort Knox, one of the largest Army posts, was less than thirty minutes away, and many military families lived in E'Town. I found my classmates to be very friendly, and I made a lot of friends, a few of which I still communicate with today through email, Facebook, and Christmas cards. I was even nominated for homecoming queen by the football player I had been dating but lost out to a local girl. Two of my good friends would also marry military men in future years, and while our husbands were never stationed at the same place at the same time, we would occasionally meet when our paths happened to cross.

CHAPTER THREE

Going to College, Meeting Ray

After my hectic high school career, I was thrilled to be going away to college and even more thrilled that I might be at the same one all four years. I did not visit any colleges during my high school years and had no idea where the best place for me would be. However, one of my friends was planning to attend Eastern Kentucky State College, as it was called at the time, now Eastern Kentucky University, so I decided to go there. Also my English teacher had recommended it, and that is how I made my choice. My parents, of course, were no help, and I was not close enough to other family members to ask for recommendations. None of them lived in Kentucky anyway. Actually, only one other family member of my parents' generation that I knew of had even gone to college, and that was just to take a few courses. In spite of my shyness and feelings of insecurity, I loved Eastern and blossomed during those four years. However, I began as a most naïve freshman.

With Daddy being the only parent working outside the home and drawing a salary, money was tight. I had worked as a secretary at the Human Resources Office at Fort Knox, KY, all summer and had diligently saved my money to go to college. I had been able to get the job by telling a little white lie that I wanted to be a full-time secretary as my career choice. I worked at this same office for the next two summers as well, always saving most of my wages to pay for my college tuition, room and board, and food. By doing so, I paid my own way through college. Since our allowance, while growing up, had been only $1 a month, Richard and I had worked at some kind of job from an early age so as to have spending money for ourselves. Richard had had a paper route; I had babysat, then worked in a dime store, then waitressed. When we first moved to Kentucky and needed money, he and I would walk along streets picking up cola bottles to take to stores for the two cents deposit money.

Before I went off to Eastern that fall of 1955, I closed out my local checking account and took all of my money with me in cash, not realizing that I could write a check on my E'Town bank account. After registering for classes, I paid for them by counting out bills from my stash of money at the appropriate window. After a few days I opened a checking account at a local bank because by then I had realized that most students had simply kept their local checking account at home and had merely written a check for their bills. I was embarrassed, but since I had not told anyone of my naivete, I did not have to suffer from others' knowledge of it.

I was very active at Eastern: I was in chorus; helped with one or two plays; was representative to the student council my freshman year; was secretary of my sophomore, junior, and senior classes; was elected to the sophomore women's honor society, CWENS; and the upper class women's honorary society, the Collegiate Pentacle; worked on the college newspaper, *The Progress* one or two years; and just overall loved being in college. I always had at least a B average every semester, at times an A- or B+; I had only 2 C's during my entire college career. Yes, I am proud of that record. I have always loved studying and learning and always wanted to teach others to love them also. I was exactly the kind of student that the faculty and the dean of women just adored! In fact, Emma Y. Case, the Dean of Women at Eastern, did not like it when I started dating Ray because she saw him as not a good student and, therefore, probably would not have much of a future. (He certainly proved her wrong!) It is true that the first full semester we dated my grades were the worst I had in college and Ray's were the best because I helped him write his papers.

Until I met Ray, my social life left much to the imagination. I was asked out some, but most of the time I ran around with one or two girl buddies. Before Ray, I had not dated anyone at Eastern for more than a couple of months. Actually, when I first went to college, I had been dating a 2nd lieutenant who was stationed at Fort Knox. He had even driven me to Eastern to start my freshman year since my dad, still the only driver in the family, had to work. However, shortly after the first semester started, my boy friend got transferred to another post and dropped me.

Ray and I met when I was a junior, and he was a senior in his fifth year at Eastern.

He likes to tell the story of how we met. It was October, 1957, and a girl friend and I were walking back up the hill to the campus from town, where we had gone to eat and get away from the cafeteria for a change. Ray's roommate was driving his white convertible, and Ray was in the passenger seat; they were headed back to campus. The two stopped and asked if we would like a ride up the hill. We recognized the car as being one we had seen around Eastern; there were not many cars on campus back in those days. So we climbed into the back seat and began to chat with the guys. When we reached our dormitory, Ray would not let me get out of the car until I promised to go on a date with him, and I finally agreed to do so. He always refers to this incident as his having picked me up off the street.

He took me to a drive-in movie on our first date and to several movies after that. He has been a movie/television buff from early on. Right after our first date or two, I came down with the worst case of flu I have ever had in my life. It was so bad that I was put into the college dispensary, and, while there, I can remember just wanting to die, I was so miserable. Ray and I were supposed to have gone to a formal dance that night, but I didn't make it, and I was terribly worried that he would find someone else while I was in the dispensary sick. I needn't have worried; he waited for me to get well. Then we dated the rest of that school year. Ray graduated in June 1958 and went to Hollywood, FL, where his folks had recently moved, to help his dad work on a boat. He entered the Army in October as a 2nd lieutenant and, after he finished his Officers' Basic Training Course, he was assigned to Fort Sill, OK, as his first duty station. We got engaged when he came through to see me in December; then we had to decide when to get married and where.

We had no one to advise us really: Daddy was in Korea at the time, so I could not easily consult him; Mother did not know what to recommend. We were in a quandary as to what to do because Ray had to leave for Fort Sill shortly, so our thinking was that we needed to go ahead and marry quickly so that the Army would move my stuff and me out there to be with him. My roommate at Eastern had gotten married in Jellico, TN, the previous year. There was no waiting—just a blood test and the purchase of a license, so we decided to follow her pattern and get married there too. Jellico is right over the TN-KY state line, so it was an easy drive. We were married in a Baptist church with a minister; my roommate and her husband were our witnesses. With Ray's parents in Hollywood, FL, Daddy in Korea, and Mother not driving, nobody in Ray's family or mine was present because of our limited time frame. When I think back over it, we did the practical, but not really the romantic thing.

What had attracted us to each other when we first met? Ray was tall, drove a red convertible, and would soon be commissioned a 2nd lieutenant in the Army—very attractive qualities for a college coed. In addition, he came from a stable family; his parents had been married since 1930 and had lived in Winchester, KY, where Ray and his siblings were born, the first twenty-seven years before they moved to Hollywood, FL. I was already friends with his sister, Phyllis, who is my age. He had lived with his grandmother on her farm in Winchester for several years after his grandfather died in order to help her manage the farm. He knew how to work hard, but he also knew how to play. For example, he taught me to jitterbug and took me to places I would never have gone by myself or with other girls. He had a lot of friends, was sociable and friendly; in short, I thought he was just right for me! When I asked Ray what attracted him to me, he said only that I was nice looking. However, I suspect that my being a serious student with the goal of becoming a teacher did not hurt either.

Ray and Darlene at Eastern, 1958

CHAPTER FOUR

My Parents' Temperaments

Chaos often occurred in our house as my parents acted out their fits of temper, and both were very adept at doing just that. I have often said that their temperaments really did not suit each other, as both were hot tempered and had argumentative natures. However, my mother would never have consented to a divorce because of her insecurity. She was not trained for any particular work and, in fact, like so many other women of her generation, she had dropped out of high school in the eleventh grade, intending to be a housewife all of her life, raise her children and take care of the house. The man was expected to be the breadwinner. The very thought that she would lose out financially in a divorce was a killer because she had no real home to go back to. That is the downside of living a military life; with all of the moves that have to be made, most of us do not have a place we can call home until resignation or retirement from the military when we can then put down roots somewhere. Even if someone, like Ray, grew up in one town until entering the military, that person may or may not choose to return there because of changes after he left or because he has found a location he likes better.

Mother was raised by Aint Eddie in Roanoke, VA, and that aunt was the only family root she had to hold onto, but Aint Eddie was getting along in years, and Mother would never have wanted to go back to Roanoke anyway. She felt as though Daddy's family, who also lived there, never liked her, and she and her two half brothers, who lived there as well, were never close. She really had nowhere to go and no income of her own to go anywhere with. I think she felt trapped many times. I know that she saw herself as different from most people because of her strange upbringing.

Her mother, Evie Warner, married three times during her short lifetime. The first marriage was to Charles William Smith, and my mother, Nadine, was born of that marriage on September 19, 1915, when Evie was only eighteen years old. When my mother was thirteen months old, Evie took Nadine to Aint Eddie's house to live with her and Grandma Warner (Evie and Eddie's mother), who was already living with Eddie. When I interviewed Aint Eddie in the early 1990s about this part of the family background, she told me that Smith had been threatening people with a butcher knife and saying that he wanted to take Nadine to live with his folks, so Evie apparently decided to get her daughter to safety by putting her in Aint Eddie's care.

After a divorce Evie ran off with John Robert Geary, who was her second husband, when Nadine was about three years old. Evie and John lived in Ohio for several years, then returned to Roanoke with their two small boys,

Jack and Dan, Nadine's half brothers. There were times when they could not afford to live on their own, so they would come to live with Aint Eddie, who would then be supporting them as well as Nadine and Grandma Warner through her work as a seamstress at Lewis-Gale Hospital. Nadine lived with Aint Eddie until she married Arthur Johnson, my father. According to Aint Eddie, my mother considered her mother, Evie, more of a sister than a mother.

The year after Evie's second husband died, she married for the third time to a much older man, probably for security. Ironically, one day in a fit of temper, he shot her and then "blew his own brains out," as Aint Eddie describes the tragic incident. This happened in January 1942 after a marriage of only three months. Evie was forty-five years old, and Commodore Perry Edwards, her third husband, was 71. One of Evie's sons witnessed the shooting and told police, according to the obituary in *The Roanoke Times*, the two had been arguing. I was only four years old when this happened, so I really never knew my maternal grandmother.

Given this kind of family background—her mother turning Nadine over to her sister to raise; her mother marrying three times, with the third husband killing her; Nadine being surrounded by women all of her life and not having a good male role model—it is no wonder that my mother lacked a feeling of security and also lacked an understanding of the male psyche. She wounded my father's over and over, saying really horrible things to him, which, in turn, egged my father on to respond in an equally hateful way to her. For a mild example, Mother might say as Daddy walked in the door late from work, "Well, it's about time. I had supper ready an hour ago. Arthur, you don't think about us waiting here for you to close up the post." She often criticized how early he went to work by saying that he had to open the post of Fort Knox, and when he came home late, saying he must have had to close it up. These words were not spoken gently; they were yelled. Then Daddy would respond in an equally harsh manner, and that spat set the atmosphere for the rest of the evening.

They both needed to see a counselor in the worst way, but most people did not go to counselors for marriage problems back in the 30s and 40s or even the 50s. They simply gutted it out, and that's what my parents did. As a result, my mother was not a happy person, and her situation became increasingly worse as she got older. She would say to us kids occasionally, "If we could just move to [somewhere that we were not living], I could be happy." When she died, along with my mourning, I thought to myself, "She can now be happy and at peace."

Daddy's background was somewhat better; at least he was raised in a more normal family situation with a mother and father, brother, and sister. As was common for my dad's generation, he had quit school in the seventh grade in order to help out his parents financially. Thus, he had to take whatever jobs he could find to earn a living to support his family after he married. He worked at various jobs, enlisted in the Army during World War II, got out after a few years, but then went back in and decided to stay, not only to serve his country but also to have a steady income. He completed his GED while in the service, as well as the equivalent of two years of college.

While we were growing up, if we needed disciplining, Daddy was the one who administered it. He did the spanking and gave us three kids the scowls and frowns to indicate we were behaving badly; I was scared of my dad but not my mother.

I remember my dad being an avid reader while I was growing up; he especially enjoyed Westerns. However, later in life as television began to be more prominent, he would watch that instead. He also enjoyed music; he had played the coronet when he was a young man and after Mother died, he would spend time ordering music CDs and listening to them.

My mother had various interests during my earlier years. She made a point of crocheting a bedspread while she was pregnant with each of us three children, and she gave us those after we were married. She also enjoyed reading love magazines such as *True Story* and and watching the soap opera *Another World*; I never saw her read an actual book. The fact that she did not learn to drive until after I had left home caused a lot of problems because it meant that anytime we had to be somewhere, we either had to depend on a friend, a neighbor, or my dad.

Another frustrating issue was that we did not have a telephone in our house during the year I was a senior in high school or while I was in college. Thus, if I needed to get in touch with Mother or Daddy, I would have to call the neighbors next door, one of them would have to run over to the house to get one of my parents, and they would have to go over to the neighbors' house to answer the phone. Since customers were charged for long distance calls based on the length of the call, my folks would have to pay for the part of the phone bill that was ours. This was back in the late 50s, and it is true that some households did not have telephones back then, but all of my friends did. Not having a telephone was a huge source of embarrassment for me, not to mention all of the trouble it caused at home. It meant that Daddy could never call home to let Mother know he would be late and that we kids could not call home either. It also meant that our friends and relatives could not call us, and if a boy wanted to ask me out for a date during my senior year, he would either have to drive by the house or see me in school. It's a wonder that I had any dates at all, but in spite of this limitation, I did manage to have several dates that year, not only with local boys but also with young Army officers that I met through friends.

Eventually, my parents did get a telephone, but it was some time after I had graduated from Eastern Kentucky in June 1959. I could have used a telephone then to find out why Mother did not make it to my commencement, turning what should have been a joyous occasion into one of the most disappointing events in my entire life. Since Daddy was still in Korea, I had expected my brother to drive Mother the two hours it took in those days to go from E'Town to Richmond. Had Daddy been in town, he would have driven them both to the commencement ceremony; that is, if he had not had to work too. Ray and I had returned from Lawton, Oklahoma, for the occasion, as I had finished my last semester by taking correspondence courses so that

I could graduate with my class. Before, during, and after the ceremony, I looked and looked for my mother, but she was nowhere to be found. Of course, without a telephone in the home, I could not call to find out what had happened. I remember that we were all invited to someone's house afterwards for refreshments and that I just burst into tears when we arrived because I was so disappointed. Here I was, the first child in the Johnson family to graduate from college, and no one in my family except my husband was there to see it.

I did not find out what happened until days later, and I don't remember if it was through a letter or how I found out. My brother, Richard, had had to work and could not drive Mother to the ceremony. I agonized over this for years because I could not figure out why Mother did not just call another family and ask for a ride. There were at least two other students from E'Town graduating with me. That is what I would have done, but, of course, my mother could never have brought herself to do that because she was just too insecure. Also, it is possible that she felt she did not have the proper clothes or wouldn't know how to act. When I later told her how disappointed I was, she said, "I know. I hated that I couldn't come; I moped around the house all day." I am sure she did feel bad about it, but I suspect I hurt a lot more than she did.

I know that my parents were proud of my accomplishment; they told me so over the years and bragged on me to their friends and neighbors, but it was hard for me to forgive Mother for this incident. I eventually did because I finally matured enough to realize that

Mother just could not handle the situation alone. As their grandchildren graduated from high school and college over the years, both Mother and Daddy were present at the ceremonies and gave generous gifts to all of them. In fact, Mother refused to mail our daughter's graduation check to her when she earned her bachelor's degree because she wanted to see Leslie's reaction to the generous amount of the check. I also think maybe she and Daddy realized how deeply hurt I was by the no-show at my graduation from Eastern.

As the years passed and the three of us children married and had children of our own, my folks did make out a will and made sure that all three of us had a copy. When they were doing something together for the good of their children, they were in agreement. In spite of their arguments, my dad provided for the family and my mother cooked good meals for us. I always knew, though, that my home was very different from that of my friends' homes, where parents seemed happier and more peaceful, at least on the surface. I never felt very comfortable inviting my friends to the house because I could not be certain what kind of mood my mother would be in. Sometimes when I came home from school, she would be fuming and ranting about something that had made her angry; other times she was calm and pleasant. These days she would probably have been diagnosed as having borderline personality or bipolar disorder, but whatever it was, she had deep-seated problems that were never resolved.

The day she suffered a massive cerebral hemorrhage, she was angry with my dad; they had just had another argument, and I'm sure she was enraged. She had sent him to a restaurant to get fish sandwiches for their supper, and as soon as he walked in the door, she came in from the back porch and started fussing at him, according to my dad's account. We don't know what she was angry about; it could have been anything. She fell in the kitchen and hit her head on the side of the table, which left a huge bruise, but that was simply a side effect of the hemorrhage, which caused the fall. She had high blood pressure, but she had cut her medication in half because she did not think she needed as much as the doctor prescribed. It was not a question of money because they got their medicine from Fort Knox's Ireland Army Hospital free of charge. Her adjustment to the prescribed dosage possibly had a bearing on the cause of her death because she may have cut it too much. She died at the age of 76 on August 4, 1992, after two weeks in the hospital, never regaining consciousness. She would have turned 77 the following month.

They had bought a small house on Lake Nolin several years before Mother died, and Daddy had started living there during the week, just coming to E'Town on the weekends. He would haul a small trailer with his riding lawn mower on it during summer months so that he could cut the grass. When we came to visit during those years, Daddy would also come to E'Town. They tried to keep up the appearance that their lives were normal, as if that had ever been the case.

After Mother's funeral my dad visited us several times in Boiling Springs and made other trips—a couple of times to Florida to watch his baseball team, the Cincinnati Reds, at spring training and to Virginia once or twice, but mostly he stayed home and watched TV, went out for breakfast (gravy biscuits) with some buddies, and smoked cigarettes. The house was so full of smoke that the walls were covered in a dingy gray film, and when the furnace came on in the wintertime, the house reeked of cigarette smoke. However, my dad was fastidious in getting all of the legal matters taken care of. He made out a new will giving the house to the three of us, he made and paid for his own funeral arrangements, and he went through the house and attic clearing out stuff. In doing so, he found various places where my mother had stashed money. I have forgotten exactly how much now, but it was hundreds of dollars. Over the years my mother had occasionally mentioned her desire to leave my dad, so apparently she was saving money in case she got up enough nerve to do it.

My sister, who lived in Louisiana, and I had planned to visit Daddy at the same time during Easter, 2001, but we ended up going much earlier when Richard, who lived in the same town, called to say they had found him dead in the kitchen of the house, apparently of a heart attack on February 15. He was 84. The irony is that all of the family thought Daddy would be the first to go because he had smoked cigarettes since he was about 12; he had had a series of stomach ailments, especially ulcers; and he had worked hard and been pretty stressed all of his life. So we were all surprised when my mother went first, but, remembering how furious she would get about the least little thing, especially something my dad had done or said, I guess we should not have been surprised.

I used to chastise myself about not visiting more often or not realizing my mother needed psychological help to get over her unusual childhood; however, I have quit that, because the truth is she had to want to be helped before she could benefit from help, and I am not sure she would ever have been willing to talk to a counselor. I know my father would not have. They did have the satisfaction of knowing that their three children were married with their own nice homes, and that gave them some pleasure before their deaths.

Arthur and Nadine during happy times in Panama

PART TWO
ARMY BRIDE

Ray and Darlene, Ft. Sill, OK, 1959

CHAPTER FIVE

First Years as an Army Bride

My first years as an Army bride were far from tranquil. Having grown up in a household in which the adult role models argued over the slightest little things, and even though I hated that way of living, I found myself following the pattern. Thus, in addition to the adjustments most newlyweds have to make, Ray and I bickered and had many disagreements over trifles. As I look back on those early years now, I realize that I was mainly at fault. I was just behaving the way I had been taught. Fortunately, Ray has always had a fairly even temperament, slow to anger, and has given me unconditional love for all of our married life.

Since we had married in the middle of my senior year of college, I still had four courses left before I could graduate, and there was no such thing as taking courses online back in the 50s! Three of those courses I took from Eastern by correspondence, but the fourth one, which was a required course for my major in English—History of the English Language, Eastern offered only in a face-to-face classroom format; thus, I took it through the University of Oklahoma, also by correspondence. That was probably the most challenging semester I had in all of my undergraduate work, but I was used to having to do whatever needed to be done because I had had to so many times growing up as an Army brat.

Therefore, the first few months of our marriage—from January through May of 1959, Ray would leave for work at Fort Sill, and I would sit at the kitchen table and do my work, which was to read, study, write responses, and mail them off, receive comments and/or grades, and do it all over again. I kept thinking to myself, "I might as well have a full-time job; at least I would be getting paid!" I did manage to do some substitute teaching during that time but not much. And when I did substitute, I felt that I was doing more "student sitting" than teaching. I had not changed my goal of wanting to teach and was looking for a job as a high school English teacher, but I was having no luck. No principal wanted to hire me because of Ray's being in the Army, which meant to the civilian population that we would be moving within a short period of time. There was also the added fact that I had absolutely no teaching experience other than student teaching during my senior year of college.

After I finished my semester of correspondence courses and graduated with my B.A. in English, I began a job as a clerk typist in the Finance & Accounting Office at Fort Sill. I was most definitely a fish out of water and a long way from entering the teaching profession. My job involved typing checks to be paid to military and civilian personnel and performing various other clerical duties. Yes, checks had to be typed on a typewriter back in those days. After a while, I was promoted to cashier, accepting payment for bills and cashing checks for military personnel and their dependents. The pay was a tad bit higher, and I enjoyed it more than I did the clerk's position. As with almost any job, I learned a great deal, met some wonderful people, and gained work experience. I was finally offered a position teaching American literature and English at a high school in Lawton, but shortly thereafter Ray received military orders to the Panama Canal Zone, so that is as close as I ever came to teaching full time at the high school level. I was going to have to wait for a full-time position until after Ray retired from the Army, and it would be at the college level.

Ray's job while at Fort Sill was as a platoon leader in an infantry battle group. His hours were long, sometimes beginning as early as 4:30 or 5 in the morning and going until 5:30 p.m. or later. Since we had only one car in those days, I would have to take him to work at some ungodly hour and either come back home to get ready to go to my work or take him and wait in the parking lot outside the Finance & Accounting Office for an hour or so until the building opened. Ray had a vast array of jobs during his almost twenty-one years in the Army—from platoon leader to executive officer in a brigade at the end of his career. In addition, he learned many skills through the various types of duties he was told to perform. At one time or another, he defended or prosecuted soldiers in a courtroom, he handled the logistics of moving large groups of soldiers to another country, he organized and carried out inspections, he was a liaison between Vietnamese and American forces, he served as a basketball coach during off-duty hours because he was tall and had played some basketball in high school, and on and on. Pretty good for a fellow who majored in industrial arts in college and one who would never amount to much, according to Eastern's Dean of Women!

Each year he and all other officers received an efficiency report, an evaluation of their work by their supervising officer, which had to be endorsed by the senior officer of their unit. Ray consistently received high evaluations throughout his Army career, but a comment on one of his first evaluations caused him to start watching his language. Hailing from the Kentucky mountains, he would say such things as "tahr" for "tire" and "fahr" for "fire," as well as other interesting regional pronunciations. He brought the enlisted men to laughter at Fort Sill in his early days as a second lieutenant when he would be in charge of the firing range. To begin firing, the appropriate command was "Ready on the firing line" and then "Fire." Ray would yell "Ready on the fahring line" and then "Fahr." Thus, in an efficiency report, his immediate supervisor wrote, "This officer is a lot smarter than he sounds." That comment definitely started Ray to work on his pronunciation of certain words. He made a conscientious effort to normalize words by saying them over and over; when he forgot, I would remind him. He made a special effort at pronouncing the words "normally" when he was on the firing range or with his fellow officers and superiors. It took more than a year before he overcame his mountain dialect by polishing his standard speech.

I discovered that social life as an officer's wife was a world apart from what I had known as a sergeant's daughter from observing my mother and daddy, who seemed to have no social obligations at all in the Army. At Fort Sill I learned about Happy Hour, that time after work, especially on Fridays, when the officers and their wives or girl friends would get together at the Officers' Club for drinks. Most of the people we knew smoked cigarettes back in the 50s and 60s, so we would have our drink in one hand and a cigarette in the other. (It makes me sick to think of it now. We both quit smoking cigarettes in 1964.) There were also "command performances," so called because every officer in the unit was expected to attend, including his wife if he were married. We, of course, attended those, many of which were formal—long dresses and gloves for the women and dress blues or whites, depending on the season, for the men.

One of the first formal functions we attended at the Fort Sill Officers' Club required the men to wear dress blues. As soon as we arrived and entered the Club and Ray caught sight of his fellow officers, he realized that he had forgotten to put all of the insignia on his uniform. Not being fully dressed with the appropriate brass was taboo, especially for a brand new second lieutenant. Leaving me at the Club to wait for him, Ray returned to the car, drove the fifteen to twenty minutes back home, put on the rest of his insignia, and drove back. That was an important lesson learned: Both of us inspected him carefully after that to make sure his uniform was all it was supposed to be.

There were also expectations of the wives, such as belonging to the Officers' Wives' Club wherever the husbands were stationed. The social activities varied, but generally there would be a coffee or a luncheon once a month. The number and kinds of events usually depended on the commanding officer's (COs) wife and what she wanted. Some COs wives were more demanding than others. Most officers' wives were stay-at-home mothers back in those days, so attending functions simply meant hiring a baby sitter and getting dressed. Crazy hat luncheons were popular back then. Women would take an old hat, usually one with a wide brim, and add all kinds of interesting things to it in order to win the Best Crazy Hat prize. I still have the one I made with a gloved hand holding playing cards. I never won the prize, however.

As is typically the case for the military, we lived in a variety of types of housing, from a tiny duplex to a large set of Army quarters. Because it was often very difficult for second lieutenants to get post housing due to an insufficient number of quarters, many military families lived in the closest towns or cities. Our first humble home was a duplex apartment at 503 ½ A Avenue in Lawton, Oklahoma. It consisted of a living room, a bedroom, an eat-in kitchen, and a bathroom—all quite small, but it was the best we could do on his 2nd Lt's salary of $333 a month. We lived there only about four months until Ray decided that it would be a good idea to purchase a mobile home so that we would have a little equity in something. We did not have enough money to even consider buying a house, nor did we have enough money for a down payment on a mobile home either, so we borrowed from Ray's grandmother in Kentucky. We paid her back monthly until we had paid off the loan.

We moved our newly purchased mobile home into a nice trailer park with a fenced-in yard, closer to Fort Sill than we had been. We lived in it about fifteen months and then decided we had better sell it because of Ray's military orders for Panama; we did not want to get stuck with a mobile home in Oklahoma and us in Panama. We sold it and moved into a rented upstairs apartment in Lawton and lived there until November 1960, when we left to drive to Kentucky to visit family and then on to New York to board our ship for the Panama Canal Zone. Thus, in our eighteen months in Oklahoma, we had lived in three different residences; this was a pattern that would be repeated but not in the Canal Zone.

CHAPTER SIX

Panama Canal Zone

Ray's Army orders to the Panama Canal Zone gave a specific reporting date in December 1960 as to when we were to be in Brooklyn to board our ship, but we decided to arrive a few days early so that we could do some sightseeing. The logic of going from Oklahoma to Brooklyn and sailing to Panama was never questioned. This was long before the Pan American Highway was built up enough to drive from the U.S. to Panama. Most of us considered it a wonderful vacation to be able to travel by ship to our overseas destinations, and indeed it was.

When we arrived in New York, we were put up at the Bachelors' Officers' Quarters (BOQ), Brooklyn Army Terminal, from which the ship would depart. While we were there, the area had one of its biggest snowfalls ever—something like 29 inches of snow. However, we went into the city often anyway and enjoyed the usual tourist attractions, even though the weather was cold.

We walked for blocks, visited the Empire State Building, saw the Christmas Show at Rockefeller Center, shopped at Macy's, ate at great restaurants, and just thoroughly enjoyed ourselves. I remember how excited I was to ride the subway for the first time and could not understand why so many fellow riders were simply reading the newspaper or a magazine instead of people watching. After a few subway trips, I understood; frequently riding the subway becomes routine and boring. When we had been there two or three days, our departure date was extended a few days, so we ended up getting a longer vacation than we expected.

I decided to take advantage of that extra time and try out for one of my favorite quiz shows: Tic Tac Dough, not the same as a later show called Tic Tac Dough, which dealt with numbers. The show I was on was hosted by Jan Murray, and it had two contestants try to make as many three- and four-letter words as possible as Jan called letters out one at a time. We had to fit the words into a 16-letter square, and the trick was that we never knew which letter would be called out next. I had watched the show and loved it. During my three appearances, I won two games before losing the third one. I won several nice gifts, including two Saks Fifth Avenue hostess gowns, two tickets to the next Orange Bowl game, a week's stay at the Hotel Diplomat in Miami, hundreds of dollars worth of Lanvin perfume and powder, and some other prizes that I don't remember. It was a lot of fun. (Ray and I were able to return to Florida after being in Panama for a few months to take advantage of the week's stay at the Diplomat, which allowed us to visit his parents, who were still living in Hollywood, FL, at that time.)

After our stay of about ten days in New York, we boarded our ship. The trip from Brooklyn to the Panama Canal Zone took several days. This method of travel was certainly one of the perks of an overseas assignment, just like being on a cruise ship, although not quite as luxurious. We did have wonderful meals and made one-day stops in Cuba and Puerto Rico. The Bob Hope Show was playing at Guantanamo Bay, Cuba, so we were able to see that while there.

As was typical during our Army career, our quarters in the Canal Zone could not have been more different from the places we had lived in Lawton, OK. We moved immediately into Quarters 99B at Fort Kobbe/Howard Air Force Base on December 27, 1960, and lived there until we left the Canal Zone in September 1963.

The quarters we were assigned consisted of a large, two-story building which contained two separate apartments, one on each side. There were probably a hundred buildings on the post like it. Each apartment had three bedrooms and a bath on the top floor; a large living room, dining room, eat-in kitchen, and a half bath on the first floor; and a carport and a maid's room with bath underneath the house. The quarters were built up off the ground with flights of stairs leading to both the front and back doors. At this time there was no air conditioning in these quarters, and I remember that the weather was so humid that the closets had heating elements in them to keep clothes from mildewing. Even the walls of the rooms mildewed. Since there was no glass in the windows, just screen and wooden louvres, the outdoors came indoors very easily. It was difficult keeping things clean, and getting help was cheap; that's why most military families hired a native woman to clean the house. Those with children had live-in maids who were paid an average of $30 a month. Since there were only two of us and no children, I had someone come to clean once every two weeks.

We also had a yard man to mow the yard and keep the weeds and plants from overtaking it. Growing plants was so easy there; you could put a stick in the ground and it would sprout. Our yard man's name was Arturo, and his favorite word was "mañana," or tomorrow in English, as in when he frequently promised he would get around to doing the yard work that needed to be done, although he rarely managed to keep his promise. However, we were to learn during this tour that life in the tropics goes at a slower pace and that "mañana" did not necessarily mean tomorrow; it just meant at some time later in the future. Ray and I learned a more relaxed way of life in the Panama Canal Zone, which was totally different from the military way of life with its structure and demands.

For example, shortly after we arrived in the country, we were introduced to another tradition of an officer's social life. We were invited to the brigade commander's home and were told that we were expected to arrive exactly on time, stay for no more than fifteen minutes, and leave a calling card in the silver tray in the foyer.

Both officers and their wives had calling cards back then, similar to business cards today. Ray was to wear his uniform, and I was to wear a suitable dress. Arriving at the door, greeting the commander and his wife, ordering a drink, sitting down and drinking and chatting, then leaving within fifteen minutes took a great deal of clock watching and guzzling, but we managed to do it. This particular rule had been relaxed quite a bit by the time Ray retired from the Army. Later the tendency was to have a "hail and farewell," usually a dinner during which the officers who have arrived to the unit recently are welcomed and those that are leaving are told good-bye with appropriate speeches and gifts.

I remember having loved being in the Canal Zone as a child with my family because I could swim year round and play outside often in the warm weather. It was a wonderful playground as I was growing up—from the middle of the fifth through the ninth grades, beautiful swimming pools on the post and impromptu ball games in the streets, but it was totally different as an adult. In addition to the heat and having two seasons—the dry and the rainy--and having no air conditioning, there was not a lot to do because the Canal Zone was quite small: ten miles wide and less than fifty miles long. In fact, soon after we arrived, we were told by our Army neighbors that when a family moves to the Canal Zone, the wife either becomes pregnant or starts drinking because of the confinement and so little to do. That is an exaggeration, of course, but some wives did have problems adjusting. Some even had affairs.

One such was my neighbor across the street, a warrant officer's wife whom I had noticed getting very chummy with the lifeguard at the officers' swimming pool on post. A friend and I watched one day as he came home with her. It wasn't too many months later that the lifeguard was shipped back to the States, and the woman had a new baby with red hair, just like the lifeguard, and with looks that were quite different from her other three children. Anything negative that a spouse did reflected poorly on the member of the military. As a child my dad had always impressed upon us the importance of being very careful about getting into any trouble, and as a wife I knew that the same policy existed, so I tried to be cautious. I cannot say that I always did everything correctly and above board, but I can say that I was never caught. After all, nobody is perfect!

We were in our mid-twenties, so we did a lot of socializing. Ray and I learned to play duplicate bridge there; we had both been playing party bridge since our college days. Actually, I had started learning to play as a freshman in high school through a friend's mother, who started bridge lessons for teenagers. (Since bridge is a lifetime learning experience, I still play occasionally and learn something new frequently.) I spent a great deal of time playing bridge in both women's groups during the day and mixed groups with Ray in the evening—both party bridge and duplicate. As always, I was involved in the Wives' Club and participated in those activities. And part of being an officer's wife was the expectation of having new officers and their wives over for dinner.

These large living quarters lent themselves beautifully to entertaining.

There was not much of a chance of getting a full-time teaching position in the Canal Zone as the number of high schools for military and civilian dependents was quite small. However, I did manage to teach part time at the Army Education Center on the post. My first teaching job was as a Spanish teacher for soldiers and their spouses. I had minored in Spanish in college; the irony was that I could pronounce the words, but I could not understand anybody's response. I had learned the old-fashioned way—reading and translating, long before the focus was on speaking the language. I was embarrassed numerous times when people who really could speak the language expected me to be fluent in it too because I was teaching it, but I was not.

It was not long until I was asked to teach English grammar and then a literature class. Again, the students were primarily soldiers and a few spouses. Even though this was a part-time job, the pay was quite good, the building was right on the post where we lived, and I gained a great deal of experience. It became very clear to me that whatever jobs I got would depend upon where Ray was assigned, and some assignments would be much better than others for obtaining work in my field.

Ray's jobs at this duty station required long hours; he was a platoon leader in Co. B, 1st Brigade, 20th Infantry, then the executive officer for the Combat Support Co., and finally the brigade operations officer. During this tour Ray was sent to the jungle warfare school in the jungle of Panama, where he learned to "rough it," living off the land, eating monkey and snake meat, walking through swamps, and hacking away jungle with machetes. The school lasted for about a month, and it turned out to be excellent preparation for Ray's first tour of duty in Vietnam a few years later. When he returned home from the jungle warfare school, he brought with him a little animal called a coatimundi. Ray delighted in having it crawl around on him, but I wasn't too thrilled with the creature. Unfortunately for him and fortunately for me, it would not eat in captivity and failed to survive.

We were in the Panama Canal Zone during two rather monumental events concerning Cuba: the Bay of Pigs invasion in April 1961 and the Cuban missile crisis in October 1962. Ray's unit was on alert during both of these events. Being on alert meant that the soldiers could be called in for duty at any time, day or night. In fact, Ray's unit spent two nights in an airport hangar with their equipment and vehicles ready to be loaded onto airplanes for a flight to Cuba during the Bay of Pigs incident. In an effort to oust Fidel Castro, President Kennedy had authorized a clandestine invasion of Cuba by a brigade of Cuban exiles. The exiles did hit the beach, but the operation was a complete failure, and Ray's unit did not have to get involved. The Cuban missile crisis occurred when the U.S. and Russia almost came to war over Russia's placing of nuclear missiles in Cuba; Ray's unit was again on alert for several days. The whole nation was on edge during this time; fortunately, the matter was resolved short of war. Both of these incidents were stressful for the military and their families living in the Canal Zone. When our tour was cut short by about three months, I was not disappointed. We left the Canal Zone in September 1963 on a ship bound for the States. Ray's new duty station was Fort Benning, GA, and we were about to enter the most hectic three-year period of our military lives.

Our quarters in the Panama Canal Zone
with Arturo mowing the yard
We lived in the right-hand side of the building.

CHAPTER SEVEN

Three Hectic Years

Ray's next assignment was to the 11th Air Assault Division, which became the 1st Cavalry Division a few months after we arrived. His specific job was Assistant Headquarters Commandant. Unable to obtain quarters on post because of so many military being relocated to Fort Benning, we rented a house in Columbus, GA, a ranch with four small bedrooms and a big fenced-in yard about twenty minutes from the post. In the 60s most homes still did not have air conditioning, and ours was no exception, so we bought a huge window unit, which a salesman assured us would be the best thing for our house. We had it installed at one end of the house, and the unit was supposed to cool the entire house. Of course, it didn't, and, furthermore, one out of three or four times that we turned it on and also had other electrical appliances on, it blew a fuse. One of us would have to go outside to the storage room in back of the house to switch the electricity back on. It was quite an experience and, like so many other of our experiences with the military, one we certainly learned from.

Even though rumors were rampant that the 1st Cav would be going to Vietnam soon, we had not been told anything definite, so when we were offered quarters on post, a single housing unit, we decided to go ahead and move in June 1965 after having lived in the house since October 1963. The quarters were really nice, not large but perfect for the two of us. Unfortunately, not long after we moved in, Ray received orders for Vietnam; he would be shipping out with his unit, the first major large force to be sent there. Many other couples and families made the same decision—that is, to move into post quarters but then received orders for Vietnam.

It was a windfall for local moving companies because once the men left, wives and children could not remain in government quarters and would have to relocate, either to Columbus or their hometowns or another city. Thus, these movers benefitted twice: the move to post and the move off post to somewhere else in the States. Obviously, I had a big decision to make: Since I had no roots anywhere, what would I do? More about my decision, but first some details about living in Columbus and working at Fort Benning.

Just as I had at the last duty station in the Canal Zone, I obtained a job working at the Army Education Center on post. My former boss knew the supervisor at Fort Benning and wrote a nice letter of recommendation for me. I taught several English classes there, but this teaching was not as pleasurable as that at Fort Kobbe had been. The classes were usually in the late afternoon in one of the government buildings which housed the Army Education Center. The classrooms had no air conditioning to ward off the hot Georgia temperatures and so were scorching and miserable for a teaching/learning environment; I had to drive from our home in Columbus to the post during the rush hour traffic; and most of the troops in the classes were not all that interested. During the 60s men could enter the Army without a high school degree, and often their military commanders forced them to take these high school classes in order to work toward that diploma. Occasionally I would have a soldier who was truly interested in earning his high school diploma, but for the most part these were men who had dropped out of school, had full-time military jobs and families, and were either too tired or too disinterested to learn English grammar. It was the worst teaching environment I had encountered or would encounter in the future, but I managed to stick with it for about a year and a half.

I developed another interest while we were in Columbus; I decided to take a modeling course with a local woman who owned her own studio, Mable Bailey. The course was several weeks long, and after I graduated I did some local modeling in stores. One day Mable called to tell me that the television station WRBL was looking for a new weather "girl" for the late night weather. I talked to Ray about it, he was supportive as always, and I decided to audition. I beat out a British woman for the job because the station manager feared that her accent would not go over well with Southerners. I did the weather Monday through Friday nights at 11:25 for nine months. Ray would be in bed asleep by the time I got home at night, but he never complained. In fact, my doing weather on local TV led to one of the stories he loved to tell over the years. He was out playing golf one day at Fort Benning with one of his buddies when a rainstorm came up. Ray and his friend went into a small shelter on the golf course, and before long another couple of men stopped at the same shelter. One of the men in the other group said loudly enough for all to hear, "That damned Darlene; she said it wouldn't rain today!" Of course, it was all Ray and his friend could do to keep from bursting out in laughter. Little did the guy know that Darlene's husband was inside the shelter too.

Being a local weather "girl" was an interesting experience which paid practically nothing--$5 for five minutes on the air, plus it took me about an hour and a half to get ready for the show. I knew absolutely nothing about the weather or weather patterns, so I called the local weather station every night before I went on the air and pulled information off the machines at the TV station. I also did a commercial for a company that I assume has gone out of business, Bev-Rich, a Kool-Aid type drink. I discovered during the taping of this commercial that the camera crew likes to try to make the person on camera "break up" or laugh. The crew filming me succeeded, which resulted in several more takes than should have been necessary. My television experience was great for learning how to be composed and how to smile in front of the camera or an audience, plus it was kind of fun to see my face, along with the faces of the newsperson and the sportscaster, plastered on billboards around Columbus and in the local newspaper. Even today people are more intrigued by the fact that I was a TV weather "girl" than they are by my having managed to earn master's and doctoral degrees in spite of all of our moves. I guess it's just human nature to be more interested in what appears to be a glamorous job rather than what some might consider a dull, academic one.

Upon Ray's receiving orders to Vietnam, I had to decide where to go and what to do. We had always thought we might like to retire to Florida; his parents were in Hollywood, where they had moved from Kentucky while Ray was still in college, and, in fact, we had bought a lot in Punta Gorda Isles (PGI), just north of Fort Myers on the west coast of the state. Actually, I had bought the lot while Ray was on TDY (temporary duty) out of town, and a sales group from PGI had come to Columbus. I happened to be at the sales pitch that the group gave because I was hired to hang around in a bathing suit, along with other Mable Bailey models. I was impressed with what the group had to say and how inexpensive the lots were. I felt we could not lose because the sales pitch was that the purchase would not be final until we visited Punta Gorda Isles and were satisfied with our purchase. Several weeks after Ray returned from his TDY assignment, we visited Punta Gorda Isles, saw the lot, and were very pleased with it. We paid $3,000 for the lot and eventually sold it several years later for $27,000, so it turned out to be a decent investment, even after paying for a seawall to be put in. Thus, I decided to move to Florida for the year Ray would be gone; that would give me the opportunity to look around. I also decided I needed more education in order to be a better teacher and to give me more options, so I applied to the University of Miami Graduate School and was accepted.

Back at the post, we made arrangements for the movers to come, but Ray had to leave for Vietnam before we could actually get moved. I remember going with him the day before his flight was to leave from Robins Air Force Base, GA, spending the night in a motel, and then seeing him off the next morning. I can still visualize him dressed in his Army fatigues, walking toward the airplane with his rifle slung over his shoulder. I realized that this type of assignment is what he had been trained for, but I was sad at the thought of what the coming year could bring and was especially scared for him, worried about whether he would come back alive or not.

In typical military fashion, I was left to make sure our furniture was packed for a storage facility, except for what I was taking with me to Florida, which wasn't much because I planned to rent a furnished place. I also had to see that the house and yard would pass inspection. Quarters had to be spic and span, including ovens and refrigerators, before a family could be released officially. We, like so many others, usually hired professional cleaners to do the job. I remember that the movers did not arrive until late in the day because there were so many families having to be moved. It was a trying day and a frustrating period of my life. We had lived in those quarters for three months—from June to August 1965—in hindsight hardly worth the move, but we, like my parents before, made the decision that we thought was right at the time.

It was a difficult year for both Ray and me, not just because of the separation but for what we were going through on opposite sides of the world. For one thing, we did not even have a quick way of communicating with each other. In 1965 and 1966 before computers and cell phones, Ray and I wrote letters and sent audio tapes to each other; it was better than nothing, but it took several days to get a letter or a tape. Back then the military had not set up a system of phone service such as servicemen and women have today. And, of course, Skype was way in the future. Plus, no television stations were interviewing military personnel overseas so that they could send Christmas greetings to their families. I am not sure we had progressed much further than we were during World War II as far as corresponding long distance, except for the addition of tapes and tape recorders for personal use. It was a very lonely year for both of us at opposite ends of the world.

Further, this first Vietnam tour was rough because the troops of the 1st Cavalry Division had to live in primitive conditions. Since they were the first large unit over there, they had to cut down jungle growth in order to build places to sleep and eat. Also, they had to trudge through thick jungle and swamps, oftentimes getting legs full of leeches; they ate C rations (food in cans, varied and very nutritious but also quite rich and heavy); they could not shower on any regular schedule; and they rarely got into a town or civilization where they could buy a good meal.

Ray, like other men stationed with him in Vietnam, was able to take a week for what was called R & R (rest and recuperation). We arranged to meet and stay at a hotel in Honolulu; I can never forget that when he walked off the airplane, I hardly recognized him because he had lost so much weight due to the demands of life in that war zone and not having regular meals. The few days we had together, though, made for a wonderful vacation for me and rest for him. We both hated to see our time together end, knowing that it would be six more months before Ray would be back in the States, and we had no idea where he would be assigned. Before I even got to Hawaii, I had a feeling we were going to have a superb vacation week because it started off great. When I reached Los Angeles for the flight to Honolulu and mentioned to the airline check-in person that I was meeting my husband, who was in Vietnam, he seated me in first class even though I had paid only for coach. I will never forget the kindness of that airline representative.

Ray was a captain when he went over and had various jobs during the year he was there. Because the Army wanted officers of Ray's rank to have the experience of being a company commander, each captain got to be in charge of a company of about 200 troops for only three to four months before someone else took over in rotation. Ray had his company for the same short period of time. Normally a company commander serves at least a year.

In September 1965 after Ray had left and I had cleared the quarters at Fort Benning, I moved into a little efficiency apartment in Coral Gables, across U.S. Highway 1 from the University of Miami. The apartment was definitely built for one person: a tiny kitchen, a tiny bathroom, and a small combination living room/bedroom with a large window that faced the major highway. By day my bed was a couch, but I hardly ever had any visitors, so that part did not really matter. I chose not to have a telephone because I did not know anyone in the area to call anyway. If I wanted to make a call, I went to a telephone booth right outside my apartment building (no cell phones yet, of course). Because my apartment building was located across from such a busy road and the university was so large, I had to drive to my classes. We had bought a British-made sports car, a TR-4, while we were in Georgia, quite a jazzy little car that continually had mechanical problems, which only added to this hectic year.

Before Ray had left for Vietnam, he had arranged to have the major part of his check sent to the bank in Hollywood, FL, where I had opened an account, for me to use as living expenses. After a month or so had passed, and no money had been deposited, I had to borrow money from his parents. I wrote Ray a letter telling him about the problem, and after two to three weeks I heard back from him to the effect that the arrangements had been properly made through the Army to send my allotment to the bank. He wrote that when he checked with the Finance Office, he was told that the appropriate paperwork had been in place from the beginning of his assignment, so the snafu (a favorite military term) was not on the military end.

Finally, after about three months of still not receiving any money, I drove from Coral Gables to the bank in Hollywood to see what the problem was. I was sitting in front of the desk of one of the bank officials, explaining the problem, when he opened his desk drawer and pulled out three checks paper clipped together. Those were the checks that were supposed to have been deposited, but they were in Ray's name instead of mine, so the bank did not know whose account to deposit them in. I could not believe it! I told the man that there probably weren't that many people named Gravett in the area and that if he had just picked up the phone and called the family in Hollywood, he could have solved the problem. (The Gravetts had settled in and around Kentucky, so there were lots of them in that state and surrounding states, but I think only Ray's parents had that name at that time in Hollywood, FL.) Of course, the banker probably did not realize there was a problem, but he should have!! This is typical of the kinds of snafus that happened throughout Ray's military career, but not only to us; others experienced various problems as well, if not with banks, then with some other business. Local folks were suspicious and cautious of those of us who did not have roots in their communities.

As if those issues weren't enough, we had a miniature poodle, Suzette, who moved with me into the apartment. However, I soon discovered that in graduate school I would be spending a lot of my time in the library doing research for the papers I was assigned, in addition to being in class. I was not home enough to take care of Suzette adequately, so I left her with Ray's mom and dad in Hollywood, which turned out to be a terrific decision. They paid lots of attention to her and spoiled her like crazy, and, of course, the dog loved it. In fact, when Ray returned from Vietnam, we chose to leave Suzette with Ray's folks, where she lived out the rest of her life in contentment. What dog would not have loved being fed cooked hamburger and rice, being brushed and combed every day, and being taken on long walks?

My social life was vastly different from what it had been in previous years as a military wife: I had none. I did meet a couple of other female graduate students with whom I did a few things, but mostly I was on my own. Basically, I studied all the time. At one point during the first semester, I became so discouraged that I decided to drop out and get a teaching job. I filled out a teaching application and was sent to an interview in a rural area well outside of Coral Gables. After driving along country roads for a while, I came to my senses and realized it would be best for both Ray and me if I stayed in graduate school. It was a wise decision.

The year became even more difficult when Ray was medically evacuated back to the States in July 1966 with a malady that caused his knee joint to swell to about three times its normal size and with his leg in a cast even though it wasn't broken. He was sent to the Fort Gordon, GA, hospital, and, with my coursework completed, I went there to be with him. He was in the hospital for more than a week and was on crutches. The doctors still had not figured out what was wrong, but he did get better. His illness would not be diagnosed until several years later. A major difficulty with military life is not being able to see the same doctor each time one goes for an appointment so that a relationship between doctor and patient can be established, and the doctor can become familiar with the patient's problems. Not only do the patients move from post to post, but military doctors rotate duty stations as well.

October 1963 through August 1966 became three hectic years for us: two moves while stationed at Fort Benning, separation as Ray completed his first Vietnam tour, my year adjusting to a tiny apartment and graduate school, Ray's medical evacuation back to the States, and so forth. I hasten to add that because we had no children, in spite of our particular problems, families with children had even more frustrations. Military life is not for the timid. In fact, we met couples, especially in Panama and later in Germany, in which the spouse could not deal with the frequent moves and being away from her folks. Flexibility or adaptability is one of the most important traits a military couple must learn.

CHAPTER EIGHT

Back to Fort Sill and then to Mississippi

Army captains must attend an advanced officers' course early in their careers; usually it is the one that is in their area of expertise. However, instead of being assigned to the infantry advanced officers' course at Fort Benning, which is what most infantry officers attended, Ray was sent to the artillery course at Fort Sill, OK. These advanced officers' courses are offered only at set times during the year, and those who are to attend are expected to arrive by a certain date. However, we were several days late arriving because of the hospital stay at Fort Gordon, GA, and a quick trip to Florida and Kentucky to visit family. Thus, instead of a larger set of quarters, we had to take what was left, which was a duplex so small that it could barely hold our furniture. However, we knew that the course was only a few months long, so, as always, we adjusted and managed, even though the dining room furniture was practically sitting on top of the living room furniture. Fresh from my graduate school experience, I did lots of reading during this period; I had a long list of "must reads."

We lived in the duplex from September 1966 to March 1967, when the entire class was sent to Fort Bliss, TX, to finish the last two months of the advanced artillery course. We rented a lovely apartment in a beautiful apartment complex in El Paso. From our apartment, we could get downtown by either driving the mountain route or the street route. We were very close to the Mexican border and went quite often to Juarez for shopping and dining. Ray's attending this particular advanced course turned out to be a great experience because I met someone whom Ray had known in Vietnam and who would become one of our life-long friends, Ron Forest. In a year or so we would introduce him to his future wife, Redon.

Ray's job was, of course, to be a student during the advanced course, and because of the limited length of time we were at these two locations, I did not attempt to find employment. It was a pleasant interlude between job assignments for Ray, except that he had to buckle down and do a great deal of studying, and a great time of socializing for me. I really relaxed during this assignment: played bridge, attended officers' wives' functions, read, shopped, and enjoyed the apartment complex swimming pool. The wives of the men in the advanced class were responsible for their own get-togethers, and since Ray was the second longest serving captain in the class, that meant I had to help out in the arranging of more functions than I normally had to deal with.

After Ray completed the advanced artillery course, he was assigned to the ROTC department at the University of

Southern Mississippi in Hattiesburg (USM), where he would be an instructor. It was not an ideal assignment because the war in Vietnam was still going strong, and college campuses in the 60s were hotbeds of anti-war protests. Male students were mandated to take military science; however, most of them did not want to do so. Military science rules required that they wear shoes and socks, but the civilian college trend was for students to go sockless. Thus, many of the students would come into class, take off their shoes, and make a big demonstration of putting on their socks in front of the instructor.

In addition to the frustration of teaching military science in an anti-military environment, Ray disliked his two bosses, one a lieutenant colonel and the other a colonel, both of whom he considered to be unprofessional. They were about ready to retire and seemed to be just putting in their time until then. Ray was a major by this time. Another difficulty was that the same medical condition that had brought him home early from Vietnam manifested itself again by continuing to flare up. Either a knee or an ankle would swell up and be painful; sometimes he had to go to work on crutches. (This condition would eventually be diagnosed as gout but not until after Ray retired from the Army and started seeing a civilian doctor in Greer, South Carolina. And it was determined that eating rich C rations during his entire first tour in Vietnam was probably what caused the gout, which is the result of too much uric acid.)

Because of the work environment and the medical problem, after eighteen months of being at Southern Mississippi, Ray volunteered to return to Vietnam. This may seem a strange decision to make, but he saw that the situation would never improve in the USM Department of Military Science as long as his two supervisors were there, and they were not going anywhere. Volunteering to return to Vietnam seemed the best option at the time; it was about the only way that Ray could get out of his current assignment, it would look good on his military record, and he figured the second tour had to be better than his first. Also we still had no children, and he knew where I would be while he was gone—at home studying, in class, or in the library. We had started trying to have a baby a few years after we were married but had had no success. As is often the case, I would get pregnant when we least expected it to happen.

Serving as Sponsors at a Military Ball,
USM, Hattiesburg, MS, 1968

I had decided when Ray first received his orders to the University of Southern Mississippi that it would be to my benefit to go back to graduate school rather than teach, this time to work on a doctorate. I have never regretted that decision because the English faculty at USM was excellent, and, although I worked terribly hard while I was there, I look back on those years of schooling now as the best learning experience I have ever had. My doctoral work and my teaching fellowship had definitely prepared me for the profession that I would enter after Ray's retirement from the military—that of college English professor.

We had rented a very nice ranch-style house with three bedrooms, two baths, living room, dining room and large kitchen in a lovely area of Hattiesburg. We moved in during the month of June 1967. So far we had managed to avoid buying a house, and we were happy about that because we had seen several military families buy homes and then be transferred within a short time. Sometimes they could not sell the house and had to rent it while they were gone with no promise of ever returning to the same location. We wanted to avoid that possibility as long as we could, and we were successful in doing so. The only purchase we made of a place to live was the mobile home in Lawton, OK, and we were able to sell that by starting early and moving into temporary housing. At the time moving again was a nuisance, but we had very few possessions in the early days of our marriage, and in the long range it was the best decision for us.

Ray's second tour in Vietnam was a vast improvement over his first. This time he was a district senior advisor to a

Vietnamese unit, and he had much nicer accommodations and a better situation all around. He had his own compound with native cooks, and he was expected to entertain his Vietnamese counterpart on occasion. Ray likes to tell the story about how the Vietnamese female cook prepared a duck one time when he had invited the Vietnamese officer over to his compound for dinner. The cook started preparing early in the day. She squatted down on her haunches, as the Vietnamese and other Southeast Asians can do comfortably, took a huge knife and beat the duck, bones and all, until everything was like mincemeat. She then cooked the meat, added spices, and put it, along with chopped vegetables, into spring rolls. Ray declared them wonderful and still remembers them fondly to this day.

After this tour of a year, Ray returned home without any apparent medical problems. However, years later, after retirement, he developed prostate cancer which was traced to the use of Agent Orange, a herbicide that was sprayed on trees and vegetation as well as food crops in Vietnam in order to defoliate them so that cover for the opposing forces would be less and their source of food would be destroyed. Agent Orange was found to cause medical problems in returning veterans, including illnesses like cancer. Ray had prostate surgery and has been cancer free since, although the surgery left other physical difficulties he has had to deal with. We believe that his first tour of duty in Vietnam was probably the main culprit, rather than his second one because he lived in fairly primitive conditions in the jungle for most of the early tour when Agent Orange was used often. The use of Agent Orange also caused health problems among the Vietnamese population.

During Ray's second tour in Vietnam, I stayed on in Hattiesburg and continued my doctoral program, completing all of my course work, my comprehensive exams, and the German and French proficiency tests. I had had a difficult time deciding which area to focus my studies on, but I finally decided to do my dissertation in the areas of 17th and 18th century British literature and have been happy with that decision. I may have been flexible in a lot of ways, but I liked for my studies to be well organized, and, thus, I loved studying the works of the authors in those areas of literature and later enjoyed teaching them: Samuel Pepys, William Congreve, Aphra Behn, Lady Mary Wortley Montague, John Gay, Jonathan Swift, Alexander Pope, Samuel Johnson, James Boswell, Frances Burney, Thomas Gray, and Oliver Goldsmith, to mention but a few. By the time Ray returned, all I had left was my dissertation; I had picked out my topic, but I was not going to get to it for eight more years!

CHAPTER NINE

Rock Island Arsenal and Washington, D.C.

When Ray returned from Vietnam in February 1970, he was sent to Rock Island Arsenal, Illinois, as a liaison officer between the military and the civilian workers there. It was a no-pressure job which enabled him to work regular daytime hours, one of the few jobs like that he had while in the Army. The Arsenal itself is one of the most interesting places Ray was stationed. It is a large island in the middle of the Mississippi River between Illinois and Iowa with a beautiful golf course and a lovely country club, privately owned by civilians when we were there but has since become public. Military assigned to the Arsenal were allowed to be members of the Club and play golf on the course; Ray and I took full advantage of the privilege.

The Arsenal is quite small in terms of employees and facilities and at that time had very few quarters for the military. Additional housing has been built since 1970. Because we could not get quarters on the Arsenal at first, we rented a duplex in Davenport, Iowa, where we lived for the next eighteen months. It was small: two bedrooms, a living room, a kitchen, and a bath, but it had a full-sized basement which served as a TV room, laundry room, and storage area, so it worked out well for us.

I thought this would be the perfect time to start work on my dissertation and began making the fifty- to sixty-mile drive to the University of Iowa for research. This was to be my work while we were here. However, before long I realized that I was pregnant. Since we had given up on ever having a child, this was a wonderful surprise. I did not want to be making that long drive, so I stopped work on my dissertation and concentrated on having a healthy baby. I lost interest in the academic side of my life temporarily. Thus, for the next several months I played bridge, attended officers' wives' functions, took long walks, and became a stay-at-home wife. Leslie Karen was born on December 6, 1970, at St. Luke's Hospital in Davenport, Iowa. Because the Arsenal had only a clinic, the Army paid for most of the cost of having her in the civilian hospital; I think our share was $25.

Unlike today, when new mothers have to leave the hospital after a brief stay, I was allowed to remain for five days, which was very helpful, considering that I had no family in Illinois or Iowa. Ray's folks were in Hollywood, FL, and mine were in E'Town, KY. Ray and I were on our own. My parents did come to visit at some point during the first few months, but they would never have considered coming to help out with a new baby the way grandparents, including Ray and I, do today. Ray's mom and dad also came for a visit when Leslie was about three months old; they stayed a few days. That was the extent of help from the family.

Since I was 33 years old and Ray would turn 36 later that December, and Leslie was born the same month in which we celebrated our 12th wedding anniversary, our lives underwent a considerable change. No longer were we free to come and go as we pleased without plans for Leslie. For the next three years I continued to be the stay-at-home wife and mother with a fleeting thought occasionally of that delayed dissertation. I had no idea when or how, or even if, I would ever get back to it.

In July 1971 we moved into Quarters #10 on the Arsenal, by far the most interesting and oldest place we have ever lived, having been built in 1899. I loved living in this house, even though it was certainly not the largest nor the nicest one we ever had, but it is a great example of the adapting skills needed to survive in the military. First of all, to get to it, we had to drive between another set of quarters and an office building as though we were going to park behind the office building. It wasn't really a street, so giving directions to visitors was always a challenge. When we got back there, two sets of government quarters were visible, a larger one, which was a two-story duplex, and then ours. Our quarters consisted of a ranch-style house with a full, unfinished basement, where we set up a double bed for us to sleep in whenever we had company. We had to enter the house through the kitchen at the back because the front of the house was just yards from the golf course, and there was not a sidewalk leading to it.

The front of Quarters #10, Rock Island Arsenal, Illinois

It was a small house, but it fit us perfectly. It had a large master bedroom, one bathroom, a huge living room/dining room combination in the middle of the house with two little rooms branching off either side of that room. One of these we made into Leslie's bedroom, which was no bigger than a walk-in closet, and the other was our TV room and Ray's painting room. He had started taking oil painting lessons while we were in Davenport and continued to paint while we were at the Arsenal. Ray got quite good at oil painting, making several of the pictures he had taken in Vietnam into paintings and doing a portrait of me. Unfortunately, this creative period of his life lasted only a few years.

This was a great assignment because Leslie was born during it, we were able to stay there for a little over three years, we had wonderful friends, we socialized a lot, we played bridge, and we both had time to play some golf. A bit of background about golf and us.

We had started taking lessons together during Ray's first assignment at Fort Sill, OK. Ray had said back then that golf was a sport we could participate in together after we got older. However, depending on Ray's job and whether or not I was working, we sometimes were able to play and sometimes not. While in the Panama Canal Zone, we both got to play quite a bit; there were beautiful golf courses there. The short time that Ray was in the Artillery Advanced Course at Fort Sill and Fort Bliss, there was little time for golf. Forget golf for both of us during Ray's two Vietnam tours, so finally at the Arsenal we both began to have time to play, and the course was so accessible that it would have been remiss of us not to do so! And thus it has been—some locations and jobs made golfing more convenient than others. Regardless, however, Ray's game got better and better, and mine never did. I am not the least bit athletic anyway. I was able to resume playing golf at the Arsenal because I could put Leslie in the nursery while I played two days a week. The nursery was conveniently located right down the hill from our house.

The weather was probably the worst part of this assignment because we had only about three months of warm temperatures—June, July, and August. We had moved from the heat of Mississippi to the colder weather of Iowa and Illinois, so we had had to adjust by purchasing heavier clothing and in other ways, such as putting a heating element in our car's engine at night when the temperature outside got too cold, even though we had a garage when we lived in the duplex in Davenport. When we moved into quarters on the Arsenal, the car had to be parked outside in the elements.

Our leaving Rock Island Arsenal was one of the most frustrating episodes we had while in the Army. Ray had received orders to go to Vietnam for a third assignment, and he had not asked for it this time. We were pretty distraught over these orders not only because of his being in Vietnam again, but here we were in Illinois, not near any family, and in government housing, which meant we had to move. Where would Leslie and I go? Again, the military problem of not having a permanent home presented itself. Fortunately, the Vietnam War ended before he had to leave, Ray requested a transfer to Germany, where I had always wanted to go, and his request was honored. Another plus was that he was promoted to lieutenant colonel before we left.

So again, we set about the business of cleaning the house to ready it for inspection; only this time we did the cleaning ourselves. We had just about taken care of all the tasks required before traveling to Germany: we had had our passport pictures taken and had received our immunizations for overseas travel, I had taken Leslie to the doctor for a final check up and had picked up her medical records as well as ours, which was the usual practice. Then in the last couple of days before we were to leave, little Leslie had been jumping on her bed when she was supposed to be taking a nap, had fallen, and had hit her head on the old-fashioned radiator in her room. I heard her loud crying, went into her room, and saw blood coming from a gash on top of her head. Back to the doctor we went; he put stitches in where she had cut herself. While we were visiting Ray's parents in Hollywood, Florida, we had to take her to the doctor there and have the stitches taken out. It is well known in military circles that Murphy's Law is alive and thriving; that is, if anything can go wrong, especially at the worst time, it will. While the members of the military are on TDY or on an unaccompanied overseas tour, something major will happen, such as the furnace going out or a child becoming extremely ill, resulting in the spouse at home having to handle the problem.

Ray's assignment in Germany was to an inspector general unit, which required him to attend a school in Washington, D.C., for a few weeks of training for the job. We rented a tiny one-bedroom apartment in a large apartment building for our stay there. Leslie slept on a cot under the staircase; she was only about two and a half years old and had learned to sleep almost anywhere.

The biggest scare I had concerning Leslie as a child took place in D.C. One day I took her out to the playground in the middle of the large apartment complex, and while she was playing on the swings, I decided to use the outdoor phone in the phone booth to call Army friends of ours who lived in the area and had invited us to come to dinner one evening. (Still no cell phones yet) However, I had left the phone number inside the apartment, so I ran back in to get it and was gone no more than two or three minutes. When I returned I did not see Leslie anywhere. Of course, I panicked and started calling her, running in the direction of the main office and asking any person I saw if they had seen a little girl. No one had. Finally, I spied her walking briskly down the sidewalk with her winter coat and hat on, heading towards a busy highway as though she were going on an errand. I caught up with her and turned her around as calmly as I could and breathed a sigh of relief. I learned a valuable lesson from that!

Leslie, age two and a half

CHAPTER TEN

Germany

Our three and a half years in Germany were by far the highlight of Ray's military career. We arrived in the country right before Thanksgiving 1973 and moved into a very large second floor rental apartment in the town of Worms, nicely furnished by the Army. (When military personnel were sent overseas in those days, they were allowed to take only a certain number of pounds of their personal belongings; thus, the government had to provide furniture.) Our German neighbors loved having a three-year-old little girl around and were constantly bringing her gifts, especially chocolate, which is a big favorite in that country. It was a challenging place to live with a small child because the apartment building was on a busy street, our apartment was on the second floor, we had to walk a few blocks to find a park for Leslie to play in, and sometimes it was difficult to find a place to park the car on the street: there was no garage or carport.

We had one interesting experience after another during our years there. One of these has to do with picking up our car in Bremerhaven, a port city in the northern part of the country. By this time the military was flying soldiers and their families to overseas locations, which meant we arrived in country faster but without a car. However, we had been in West Germany less than a month when we received word that our car had arrived. We were excited about finally having our own means of transportation again and not having to depend on Ray's co-workers and their wives to take us around--Ray to work and me to the commissary and PX. Also we had been looking forward to our first European train ride and to sharing a compartment with Germans and listening to them speak their language, which we were trying to learn. So early one typically cold, sunless, German December morning, the three of us boarded a train which would take us to Köln, where we would switch to a train headed to Bremen, and then switch trains again to one headed for Bremerhaven.

Heeding friends' advice, we had purchased first class tickets. After we boarded, we hunted for an empty compartment, found one, and settled ourselves by the windows to take in as much of the German countryside as possible. It was not long before a nicely dressed, somewhat elderly man took one of the three remaining seats, and the train departed promptly on schedule. One can generally set a watch by the arrival and departure of German trains; they are that punctual.

As the trip progressed, Ray and I made small talk between ourselves and enjoyed the beautiful view of vineyards on one side and castles along the Rhine River on the other. Not yet having had the chance to learn much

German, we did not attempt to communicate with our fellow passenger, who appeared to be dozing most of the time anyway. At least he did not seem to notice when Leslie opened her Peanuts lunchbox and began eating her lunch about 9:00 a.m.

I had memorized one German sentence which I knew I would need, and it was not long until Leslie was tugging at me. Beckoning to a passing porter, I inquired, "Wo ist die toilette?" After I had repeated the question four times, with the porter questioning me back each time with "Bitte?" our elderly gentleman passenger put his hearing aid in and assisted until I finally made myself understood to the porter and got the directions I needed to take Leslie to the bathroom. Ray said I spoke too timidly to the porter; he probably looked at me as an American and assumed I was speaking English. Of course, he might have been hard of hearing too. "Toilette" is very similar to "toilet," so my shyness in speaking German must have been the problem. It embarrassed me, but I learned to speak German with more confidence as a result of the incident. It turned out that the elderly passenger was German but spoke beautiful English. We conversed with him the rest of the way to Köln.

After our final change of trains in Bremen, we found ourselves in an empty compartment except that there was one large suitcase with an enormous package on top of it in the luggage area above the seats. We realized that someone must be sitting there already, but we hoped it would be no more than three people. After a half hour or so, in came a friendly looking man, probably in his 40s. Again, assuming he spoke only German, we refrained from making any conversation with him, but we talked with Leslie and between ourselves and exchanged pleasant glances from time to time with the stranger. After a half hour or so, the man brought some coins out of his pocket. Holding them in his hand, he leaned towards Ray and asked in perfect Long Islandese, "Do you know if this will be enough to make a call in Bremerhaven?" Ray and I nearly burst out laughing and enjoyed chatting with this New Yorker all the way to our mutual stop, Bremerhaven. We had not overheard any of our fellow passengers speaking German, but we had had two interesting conversations in English on our German train.

Another memorable experience occurred when we were invited to have cake and coffee at one of our German neighbor's apartments in the same building in which we lived. The daughter of one of the families had announced her engagement, and the wife of the Housmeister had collected money from each of the other six tenants in the building and bought a joint gift for the newly engaged couple. As a thank you, the girl and her family invited us all to their apartment for cake and coffee at 4 on a Saturday afternoon. It had long been a German tradition to have cake and coffee at 4 or 5 in the afternoon.

At the appointed time Ray, Leslie, and I appeared at the door of our host's apartment, with Ray dressed in a coat and tie, just like the other men. After a bit of conversational small talk, of which Ray understood nothing, and I understood only a little, we all sat down at the table for refreshments. Our hostess wheeled into the room a cart which was laden with not one or two, but three different kinds of cakes, plus assorted cookies and pastries. We were invited to select one, and it was served to us, followed immediately by a cup of freshly brewed, delicious coffee. Europeans have a way with coffee that has finally been picked up by Americans. It comes out flavorful, full-bodied, aromatic . . . and it tastes wonderful.

As I finished my piece of cake and was getting ready to relax and go back to trying to understand the conversations around me, I noticed that when the other guests finished one piece, they were being offered another and taking it. I had always been taught that taking more than one piece of cake was rude. However, here it seemed to be the thing to do, so I selected my next piece, and the hostess served it to me. I could barely finish that one, but as I did, I looked around and saw that Ray and a couple of the other men were accepting their third pieces!

Thus, I discovered, after several other cake and coffee hours, that the custom was as follows: There is always a selection provided, and one continues to select and eat as long as he or she likes. Even at birthday parties—both children's and adults'—a hostess would never offer just one cake as we Americans do. One reason that Germans can eat so much cake is that theirs is more nutritious, has fewer calories, and is not as sweet as our typical American cakes. Their cakes are oftentimes tortes with unsweetened whipped cream or one-layer cakes with congealed fruit toppings. It was not unusual to walk into a hotel bar in Germany during what we U.S. citizens consider "cocktail hour" and order a drink, only to see people sitting around having cake and coffee.

We disappointed our German landlord greatly when we moved into government quarters in Worms in June 1974, after having lived in the apartment only seven months. I personally felt guilty leaving again so soon. Our landlord lived in another town in Germany and had come to visit us after we had moved in, bringing a big bouquet of flowers. It was obvious that he was pleased with his us as his new tenants, but once again we made the decision that we thought was best for us at the time. We moved because we thought that the government quarters we were being offered would be an ideal place for us during the remainder of Ray's assignment in Germany, not knowing the plans the Army might have for us in the near future.

Our new quarters were spacious, on the ground floor, and in a group of quarters among other military families who had small children. The best part for Leslie was the playground with a sandbox beside our building and having children her age to play with. This was an ideal situation, so, of course, it did not last long. Ray's unit moved to a military post near Kaiserslautern, so we had to leave those lovely quarters after five months. We rented the main floor and upstairs of a house in a little town near Kaiserslautern called Fischbach.

Our landlords, Jakob and Irene Eberle, lived in two rooms in the basement with their two teenagers, while we occupied the main part of the house. They had built the house with the objective of renting it out to a military family. It was a lovely, modern house: the downstairs floor had a kitchen, living room, dining room, and small bathroom, and the upstairs had three bedrooms and a bathroom. We lived here from November 1974 to May 1977 and found it to be a fascinating experience. We were surrounded by German neighbors, and Jakob and Irene left fresh brochen (fresh rolls, crusty on the outside and soft on the inside) at our doorstep every Saturday morning. We would take walks around town and into the woods on Sunday afternoons, which our German neighbors also liked to do. But most of all, it was great to be settled in one place for two and a half years. We had moved so much since Leslie had been born that by the time she was four years old, she had had five different bedrooms in various residences, not to mention temporary places that we stayed a few nights here and there. Maybe that's why she can fall asleep anywhere to this day!

From the time we first moved in, we had often noticed our landlord out back watching over a long rubber hose which seemed to be sucking up dirty water of some kind from a four- foot by four-foot hole in a concrete portion of the yard. He would then let it spew into a field in back of the house. A foul odor always accompanied this event. Ray suggested that the hole might be a holding tank of some kind, sort of like a septic tank but missing the pipes that go out in different directions underground. We did not believe it was, though, because we did not think that someone would pump out a tank like that and let the foul water go into the field.

One night, however, while we were having a mixed German-English chat with the Eberles, we discovered what the business was all about and how we were contributing to it. Ray's holding tank guess was absolutely correct. The landlord, along with many other German homeowners in the smaller towns, would pump out into the fields whatever goes into the toilets. With two bathrooms in our part of the house and only one down in the basement, we were probably contributing the larger part of the stuff. That evening, Frau Eberle, being more assertive than her very quiet-spoken husband, commented on the frequency with which they were having to pump out the holding tank. We all wondered at this until she followed up by asking where our washing machine hose emptied out.

A bit of explanation is needed here. The house was not rigged properly for an American washer because of the two-faucet requirement. So the landlady had a German washer installed in the upstairs bathroom where there was a cold water faucet and a plug. German washers back then (and maybe they still do) took in only cold water and heated it to the temperature called for by whatever button has been previously punched by the operator. At the time that the machine was installed, the landlady had told us to run the drain hose into the bathtub. However, Ray decided later that since the toilet was right next to the washing machine, it would be the more convenient receptacle. Thus, whenever I washed clothes, I just hooked the drain pipe over the potty seat, and the process seemed to work fine. German toilets were different from American ones in that water did not accumulate in the bowl and sit there until flushed. There was very little water to begin with, and the hole was quite large so that whatever was poured into it went straight on down.

When Frau Eberle had asked where the washing machine hose was emptying out and I responded "the toilet," it became clear what we had been doing for the past several weeks to our poor landlord by having the dirty water from the washing machine (probably equivalent to maybe 20-25 toilet flushes) drain into his holding tank three or four times a week. We promptly switched the drain hose to the bathtub, from which the water drains into a ditch out in back of the house, and felt very guilty for our being responsible for Herr Eberle's holding tank woes.

As delightful as living in the small town of Fischbach was, there was the problem of having to drive several miles on the autobahn to get to the commissary and PX; plus, Leslie did not have too many children to play with where we were. Many of the residents were older with grown children; there was only one other American family living there, but their house was at the other end of town, and they weren't too friendly anyway. The one child that was the nearest to her was a little German boy, Gunter, who was all boy and not the nicest one either, but she did learn some German from him. I took her to the nursery school in the military compound called Vogelweh so that she would have more children to play with.

When it was time to start kindergarten, she had to go to Sembach Air Force Base, which was quite a distance away and required a school bus ride. She had to be at the bus stop around 7:30 in the morning, and it was at the end of our little town, about a mile from our house. I would ride her on the back of my bicycle to the bus stop and pick her up again when the bus brought her back. I felt right at home doing this because so many Germans rode bicycles. Fortunately, Leslie has always been a morning person, so she had no trouble getting up early for what was sometimes a chilly ride on the back of Mom's bicycle.

The Inspector General's Office to which Ray was assigned was charged with inspecting Army units all over Western Germany and parts of Great Britain. For the last part of our tour in Germany, he was the Inspector General in charge of the other officers, NCOs, and civilians who worked in the office. He made the assignments, and he also traveled himself. In fact, he was gone an average of two to three weeks out of four. That part was difficult, but because he knew his schedule at least a year ahead of time, we were able to take many trips all over Europe, as well as learn to snow ski, a sport we would enjoy for years to come.

Because I had arrived in Germany ABD (all but dissertation), I was able to get a part-time teaching job almost immediately. I taught high school-level classes at the Army Education Center and college-level courses for the University of Maryland, both in Worms and in Kaiserslautern. Again, most of my students were military personnel and their dependents. I was able to use the training I had received while working on my doctorate at Southern Mississippi and, thus, gained a great deal of experience, which was an asset when I started teaching full time after Ray retired from the Army.

Darlene, Leslie, and Ray in Germany

CHAPTER ELEVEN

Skiing and Traveling in Europe

Not long after we arrived in Germany, new friends we had met there, Bill and Sondra Rosenthal (he was also with the Inspector General's Office where Ray worked), encouraged us to go with them on a ski trip. So in February 1974, about three months after we had arrived, we went skiing for the first time in Kirchdorf, Austria, to try it and see how we liked it. I did not take to it too well at first; Ray did better than I did, just as he has done with golf. We learned the basics, and I liked the baby slope but was scared of the big slope. Ray fell and hurt his knee the first day trying to get up after a fall, which we discovered is a skill that has to be mastered.

After that trip, Bill and Sondra persuaded us to go with them to the Swiss Ski School in Wengen, Switzerland, in December 1974, where we received a week's training with classes of different levels. We rented a chalet in the mountains where we cooked our own meals. It was a beautiful location and an eye-opening week. The town of

Wengen was—and I am sure still is--beautiful, right in the heart of the Alps; we had to take a cog train to reach it. (A cog train is one that climbs a steep mountain; the rail has cogs engaged by a cogwheel on the train to ensure traction.)

The first day on the slopes at the ski school, everyone was taken to the mountainside and told to ski down one at a time. Based on how we skied, we were put into classes. There were seven levels, and I was definitely a beginner and was put into Level I; Ray was smart enough to realize that if he got in the beginner's class, he would be sidestepping up the mountainside half the time, so he practiced and managed to get into a higher level class. I soon discovered the error of my ways, for the beginner's class had Max as a teacher, an older man, who enjoyed stopping for coffee. We spent most of our time sidestepping halfway up a slope and then skiing a little ways down before stopping and doing the same thing again with lots of coffee breaks. In the meantime Ray's group was skiing all over the mountainside. However, I wasn't totally disappointed because I was not sure how much I was going to like this new sport. (At this stage we were renting skis and boots, which were not that comfortable. After we had skied a few times and purchased our own gear, I liked the sport better.) At the end of the week there was a big race in which everybody participated, and we all received medals for participation, which was a good thing because I would not have gotten a medal otherwise.

After this, we went on many ski trips to Austria and Switzerland. We began taking Leslie with us during her fourth year, putting her in the kindergarten class. She caught on fast and loved it. The biggest problem was making sure she had gone to the bathroom before she put on all of the skiing gear—ski suit, gloves, mittens, ski hat, boots, skis. There were many times when she would wet herself, and we would have to take her back to our room or apartment, take her clothes off, and start all over again. I remember being a bit frightened the first time I saw her going up on a chair lift in a seat all by herself, along with other four- and five-year-olds. However, it was such fun watching all of them ski down the mountain behind the ski instructor like a flock of baby ducks following after mama duck.

Skiing in the Alps was quite an experience in many ways. For one thing, the mountains seem to go on and on forever. In Switzerland we could actually ski from one small town to another. On many of the slopes there would be restaurants where we could stop for a coffee or gluh wein (hot, spiced wine) or lunch, for that matter. I remember that to get to some of the mountains in Europe, we would have to take a cog train, such as the one to Wengen. I also remember skiing over to another town and not knowing how to return to our original location. It took asking and skiing and a bus ride to return to where we were staying.

One of our most harrowing experiences occurred in Switzerland when we were going up a T-bar lift. I was on one side of the T-bar, and Ray was on the other side with little Leslie between his legs with her skis inside his. All of a sudden we started drifting to the left, and before we knew what had happened, we had all been dropped off the left side in deep snow with our skis half buried in it. Ray and I had a terrible time getting back up; we all just laughed, but we could not get back to the T-bar in the deep snow and had to ski over to a different slope. We had several scary incidents happen, such as falling off the chair lift as we were trying to disembark at the top of a slope and scurrying to get out of the way before the skiers behind us in the next chair had to get off, falling on my rear end and coming home with a huge black and blue bruise all over it, and the back tip of a ski getting hit by a snow boarder or a too-fast skier, and other similar escapades.

The last ski vacation we took in Europe was during the Easter weekend in 1977, when Ray, Leslie, and I went back to Wengen, Switzerland. Ray and I had wanted to go back one last time to the place we had enjoyed so much. We rented a small chalet on the mountainside and had a lovely snowfall awaiting us Easter morning. I remember Ray taking a picture of Leslie and me with her Easter basket sitting out on the snow. For her age of six years, Leslie was a good skier, and we had a great family skiing vacation.

During our stint in Germany we took a great number of trips, made easier because Ray knew his schedule well in advance and I was teaching only part time and could take time off between semesters. The Army's generous leave (vacation) policy also helped tremendously. Each soldier from a private to a general gets two and a half days leave per month, which amounts to thirty days a year; weekends are included in the leave count though. However, a soldier can accrue up to sixty days. Ray never let his leave accrue that much, especially while stationed in Germany.

In addition to Germany, Austria, and Switzerland, Great Britain was one of the countries we visited more than once. One of our favorite trips to the British Isles came later in our Germany tour when we traveled to both Scotland and England with the intention of playing golf in the country that is the home of the sport. We drove the old second- or maybe third-hand Volkswagen that Ray had bought not long after we had moved to Germany and spent the first night near Charleville, France, before going on to Calais, where we crossed the English Channel on a ferry. We spent the first night in England in the pretty little town of Stamford, only the first of several overnight stays in small, lovely old towns in which a full breakfast came with the room.

On our way to St. Andrews, we visited York, Edinburgh, and the wee town of Auchtermuchty, which we would have had trouble finding if a kind Scotsman had not led us there and introduced us to the owners of the Boar's Head Inn. Our guide insisted on buying us drinks and talking to us, but his accent was so thick that Ray and I could hardly understand a word the man said; however, we both were awed by his hospitality. We spent the night in the inn and, after a wonderful breakfast, left the next morning for St. Andrews, where we stayed at the St. Andrews Hotel. Our room had a beautiful view of the golf course, the North Sea, and the Royal and Ancient Clubhouse. We both played the Old Course the first day; I spent a lot of time in the bunkers, or sand traps, which were so deep that I could not see over the ridge while I was trying to hit my ball out. I am sure my caddy was laughing his head off, but that was OK because

I have been able to say that I played the course where golf started.

We visited many castles and spent the night in a hotel overlooking Loch Ness but never saw the monster. We continued wending our way through England; Ray played one more golf course, Gleneagles, but after that we decided there was too much to see to spend our time playing golf. We stopped at more castles, drove through the Lake District, went to Canterbury, then to Dover and a visit to Dover Castle. On our return from England, we crossed the English Channel by Hovercraft in thirty minutes this time as opposed to the two-hour ferry crossing coming over. We spent one night in France, just as we had at the beginning of the trip, and then drove on home. It had been a wonderful twelve-day trip.

On these long trips, and even on some of the shorter ones, we generally left Leslie with friends who had children. Our feeling was that at 4, 5, and 6 years of age, she was better off in school than traipsing around Europe with us, since she would be bored with the narrated tours, the sightseeing, and the other adult things we like to do while traveling. The ski trips were a different matter because we all three enjoyed skiing; we usually took her with us on those.

We took two more long trips while we were in Germany: a ten-day one to Spain and a two-week one to Italy. The trip to Spain was through American Express, which ran a travel agency near where we lived. This trip took us to Madrid, where we witnessed a bull fight, Cordoba; Seville; Granada; Toledo; and Barcelona. With only twenty participants we received plenty of individual attention and had a terrific guide with us the entire time. One of the group members was of Spanish heritage and spoke the language fluently. We linked up with her and her husband and did things together, including going to restaurants. She and I made a good pair because I could read the Spanish menu and translate it better than she could, but I could not make myself understood when I spoke. So during the whole trip, she did the speaking and I did the reading and translating.

It is hard to believe that five months after that trip we took a trip to Italy, this time with another Army couple, Pete and Rosemary Rizzo. Both of us drove Volkswagens and followed each other, which turned out to be quite challenging in the big cities with lots of traffic, such as Rome and Naples. This trip was full of interesting experiences, especially with our car, that same Volkswagen we had taken to Great Britain. Both cars leaked and took on water when it rained on us all day the first day of the trip; we had to stop and buy large sponges to soak it up. We spent the first night in Innsbruck and left the next morning, crossing the Italian border and driving through the Brenner Pass, viewing absolutely breathtaking scenery along the way—mountains with picturesque villages scattered all over and running brooks below with higher snow-covered peaks in the background. Perched atop many of the mountains were old castles, which appeared to be in very good condition. It was only the beginning of what was to be one of our most exciting trips.

We were in the country for two weeks and visited or stayed in such sites as Venice, where the residents had boats parked in their garages the way we Americans have cars; San Marino, a medieval walled city that sits atop a cliff; Rome, where we visited all of the main tourist attractions and were able to see Pope Paul VI at St. Paul's Basilica during one of his weekly audiences and hear him give an address in five languages; Naples, from which we took an all-day tour to Vesuvius and Pompeii; Siena; Volterra; Tirrenia; Pisa; and Florence. We bought a whole car load full of treasures in Italy: marble-topped end tables, statues, paintings, leather boots and gloves, and much more. When we left Germany we had two small suitcases in our Volkswagen; when we returned we had a car bursting at the seams.

Like most lengthy trips, this one was not without its problems. The four of us took turns having upset stomachs and feeling ill on various days. It wasn't until we returned home and told others about this malady that we learned the reason why. Italian restaurants at that time did not always have water hot enough to sterilize the dishes, so bacteria could still be present, plus the fact that the serving dishes were not always washed after being used. I remember seeing the waiter at one restaurant, after removing our soup bowls, take the serving plate underneath the bowl, wipe it off with a dish towel, and put it back on the stack of dishes to be used again.

Another problem that continually arose had to do with our old Volkswagen. The day after our trip to Venice, we got off to a late start because our car had a gas leak. Ray and I walked to the VW garage and got the necessary part, and Ray fixed it. However, the conversation at the garage was challenging because the mechanic knew no English;

I had worked on my Italian before the trip but did not know the words for car parts, so he and I finally ended up communicating in German, which I knew a lot better than Italian.

We took several more trips while we were in Germany, both short trips within the country and longer trips to other countries. In the country we visited Heidelberg Castle more than once; Rothenburg, a medieval walled town, where we spent the night in a farmhouse with a barnyard smell, slept on feather beds, and had no heat even though the weather was still cold in April; Bavaria, one of the loveliest places in Germany, where we visited King Ludwig II's castles: Herrenchiemsee, Linderhoff, and Neuschwanstein, my favorite with its swan motif; Oberammergau, the center for German wood carvers; a Rhine River cruise; Trier; Idar-Oberstein, which has a church carved out of the side of a mountain; Nuremburg; and lots of others.

A very different trip was the one to West Berlin with Pete and Rosemary Rizzo, which we took in October 1974. Germany was still divided at this time, with East Berlin under Communist control. Ray and Pete were not allowed to enter East Berlin because they were American Army officers, but Rosemary and I took a guided bus trip there. While West Berlin had been almost totally rebuilt after the end of World War II, East Berlin had not. We saw few vehicles on the main roads, many crumbling buildings, and lots of debris all along our bus route. The difference between the two Berlins was hard to believe. It is no wonder that all Berliners, but especially those living in the

East, were so excited when the Berlin wall came down in 1989 after separating the two Berlins for 28 years.

As for trips outside of Germany, we traveled to Holland and stayed in Amsterdam but visited Alkmaar, well known cheese market; Aalsmeer, a flower market; the Hague; Madurodam, a large miniature town; Delft, where Delft Blue pottery is made; and Rotterdam. Ray and I also traveled to Paris for a week's stay and took in all of the usual tourist places—the Louvre, the Eiffel Tower, the Place de Tertre, as well as various museums. In spite of Paris being a beautiful, lively, and exciting city, this was not a very good trip. We found Parisians to be most unhelpful to Americans who did not speak French, and that has always been my worst language. The year was 1975, and at that time we still had American military stationed in France as a result of World War II. It wasn't long after that, however, when the U.S. pulled its military out of the country at France's request. When Ray and I took a group trip back there in 1997, we found a much friendlier attitude.

My final trip outside of Germany was to Greece with another Army wife; Ray said he was tired of traveling! This was an interesting and educational trip for me because we toured so many of the places that I would teach about later in world literature, such as Athens, Corinth, Delphi, Mycenae. As opposed to the Parisians, the Greeks loved Americans, especially Greek men, who seemed to adore American women and would run up to us on the street, asking if we knew their friend "Sam" or "Joe" in Boston or something similar.

It is easy to understand why we considered our tour in Germany to be our favorite. Not only did we learn about the German culture and get to travel to so many exciting places, but Ray had a great job and I had the opportunity to teach. It was also a wonderful experience for Leslie, although she probably does not remember much about it, since we arrived over there when she was three and returned home when she was just shy of six and a half years. Because we had loved being in Germany so much and because Leslie was now in school and we did not want to move her in the middle of a school year, we extended our three-year assignment another six months and returned to the States in May 1977.

Our home in Fischbach on Harztahlerstrasse

CHAPTER TWELVE

Fort Benning, The Final Assignment

Ray's last assignment was at Fort Benning, GA, where he was the Executive Officer, Headquarters, 197th Infantry Brigade. This was a high profile position, second in command to the full colonel who was the brigade commander, a position Ray never thought he would have, so it was ironic that this would be his last position in the military. It was also one with fairly regular hours, except for the year that the whole unit went on winter exercises to Fort Drum, NY, and had the challenge of dealing with several feet of snow. We thoroughly enjoyed being back at Fort Benning and especially loved our post quarters.

Fort Benning is a large Army post that has all of the amenities found on the other big bases in the U.S. In addition to several Army units, it has a large and complete hospital, a well-stocked commissary and post exchange, a dental clinic, elementary schools, a library, very nice officers' and non-commissioned officers' clubs, housing for both officers and NCOs, as well as all the other services one would expect. In addition, after we moved into quarters on post, Ray was close to his office, and Leslie was within two blocks of her school, so she could ride her bicycle. Because we had moved so often, it was hard to remember our new address and phone number for the first few days after we arrived in another place, so I would write that information on two pieces of paper. One piece would go with Ray to his new job where he always had to fill out lots of forms, and the other one would go to school with Leslie.

As usual, there were no government quarters available when we first arrived, so we rented an apartment in Columbus for a couple of months until housing on post became available. In July we moved into a big, beautiful set of quarters: a house of two stories with a full basement, three large bedrooms, two baths, a large room off the master bedroom surrounded by windows (which I used as my study and in which I finished my dissertation), and a small extra room upstairs, which Leslie used to tap dance and play in. Downstairs were a wide hallway with a big dining room and eat-in kitchen to the left from the front entrance and to the right a very large living room with a small room beyond it which could be a library or a music room, and a room off the living room surrounded by windows which we used as our television room. It was a home made for entertaining and by far the nicest place we had ever lived.

The only two downsides to it were that it was on a very busy street, and the garage was at the end of the backyard, which meant carrying groceries quite a distance. We entertained a great deal here with both large and small dinner parties. In his position Ray had many people working for him, we were expected to entertain, we were used to it, and we enjoyed doing it.

408 First Division Road, Fort Benning, GA

When a military family moved into government housing, the rule was that the family would not do anything permanent to the quarters. If the walls needed painting or a new light fixture or a new anything, one had to call the appropriate office. Therefore, one did not paint rooms different colors because there was one standard paint color for all quarters; one did not install carpeting because if the Army wanted you to have carpeting, they would have installed it; one did not put nails in the walls unless you were sure you could fill them in so that they would not be noticeable when you moved—toothpaste was one of the favorite fillers. Therefore, military families' homes were quite similar except for the furnishings; overseas they were even alike in the government-provided furniture. In this particular set of quarters, the hardwood floors were old and scratched, so we bought inexpensive carpeting and just laid it on the floor without any padding. That's what many families did. Improvising was a key word in the military.

For the first few months after settling in, I did some part-time teaching for Troy State University at Fort Benning and for Chattahoochee Community College in Phenix City, AL. But it wasn't long before I started thinking more and more about that uncompleted dissertation and talking with Ray and my friends about it. I had thought of moving the family back to Hattiesburg, MS, after Ray retired and working on it then, but a friend, Linda Larson, whom I had known in Germany and whose husband had also been transferred to Fort Benning, asked, "Why wait? Why not work on it now and have it finished when Ray retires?" That question made sense. However, I had left USM in February 1970, and here it was 1978; furthermore, I had not done a thing on it since we had lived on Rock Island Arsenal in 1970. Usually there is a time limit for completing a doctorate once a person starts one.

I figured I had nothing to lose by inquiring, so I checked to see if my topic was still available (that is, no one else had written a dissertation on it yet), and it was. I wrote the chair of the English department and laid out my situation, where all we had been, what all had happened, and how I would like to be allowed to complete my dissertation and would be willing to take additional courses if necessary. I attached a little picture of myself at the bottom of the letter in case the faculty had forgotten me. Apparently, I had not been forgotten; I received a wonderful letter back telling me that I should forge ahead and naming the professor who would be directing my dissertation, Dr. Linwood Orange, who had taught me several courses during my doctoral studies. This letter was a huge relief, and I was pleased with the person named who would be working with me; he would be a good mentor because he was both knowledgeable and a detail person.

Instead of teaching any more classes, I spent the next year working on the dissertation, and that became my job. After Ray left for work and Leslie left for school, I worked diligently on it every day. I had gotten permission to use the library at Auburn University in Auburn, AL, which was about fifty minutes away from our quarters. I drove to Auburn several times during the first few weeks because I had to copy the original text of the 17th century play on which I was writing a critical edition. It was on an old micro-card, and there was no way to copy it back in the 70s other than to type the entire play word for word as it appeared on the card, which was quite tedious. Since this was before word processors, it meant hauling my portable electric typewriter each time I made a trip to the library at Auburn. It took five or six trips to complete the typing of the full play, each time with my driving to Auburn, trying to find a parking place, lugging my heavy electric typewriter down to the basement, and sitting all day and typing. Other than trips to the Auburn library to do research and to check out books, which the university very kindly gave me permission to do, I did most of the work at home in that room beside the master bedroom in our beautiful quarters.

Ray had decided that he would retire sometime in 1979 as a lieutenant colonel for several reasons. We wanted Leslie to grow up in one community and not have to go through the kind of turmoil that I had gone through in changing schools so often. Second, promotion to full colonel was difficult to achieve, and we did not want to stay on a few more years just to be disappointed. Ray had always been promoted on schedule in previous years. Third, I was more than ready to start my college teaching career. Finally, we were just plain tired of moving.

Therefore, at the same time I was working on my dissertation, I was applying for college teaching positions. I sent out about ninety applications and received only one interview, at a small two-year college, North Greenville, in Tigerville, SC. It was really not surprising that faculty search committees and deans did not jump at the chance to hire me: Here I was a forty-two-year-old woman who had not had one year of full-time teaching experience and who had been a "camp follower" for the last twenty plus years (as in olden days when women followed their men from camp to camp). However, this college dean took a chance on me, and when I was offered the position, even though the salary was much lower than what I had hoped for, I accepted. I remember my dissertation advisor telling me, "Don't get hung up on salary; just get your foot in the door." And that's what I did. I successfully defended my dissertation at USM and received my Ph.D. degree in August 1979. My dissertation title is *A Critical Edition of*

Abraham Cowley's "Cutter of Coleman Street." Abraham Cowley (pronounced Cooley) was a 17th-century poet and playwright, and this particular play had several different versions. My task had been to compare all of them, each word and punctuation mark, write an introduction giving the background to the play and placing it in literary history. All of which must sound terribly dull to the average person, but I loved working on it, probably because it required intensive detailed work, and I love details.

It had been one tough year, but I had been determined to get this degree. Besides, according to Ray's theory, I was the one who was supposed to start working when he retired! He had declared early in our marriage and had continued to say often to family and friends that he was planning on working the first twenty years and that I was going to work the next twenty. This statement caused amusement to everybody, including the two of us. Amazingly enough, though, his theory became partly fact, except that I ended up teaching full time for 28 years with several years before that of teaching part time.

PART THREE
CIVILIAN

Darlene in academic cap and gown,
beginning a full-time college teaching career at age 42

CHAPTER THIRTEEN

Adjusting to Civilian Life

After moving seventeen times in almost twenty-one years, we left Fort Benning and the Army in July 1979, moving into temporary housing on the campus of North Greenville College, now University, in Tigerville, South Carolina, where I had been hired to teach English. Neither of us had ever lived in this state. The college had made arrangements for us to stay in a little apartment on campus while we were house hunting, and it was pretty dismal: no hot water the first night and only one bedroom, so Leslie had to sleep on the floor on two couch cushions, but, of course, this situation did not bother her as she was used to falling asleep anywhere.

Fortunately, we were there only a month; we moved into our beautiful house in Taylors, SC, in August, the first house we had ever owned after 21 years of marriage.

We entered this new phase of our lives without any idea of what it would cost us to live as civilians. While in the military, Ray had received a monthly stipend, a so-called housing allowance, as part of his salary to help defray the cost of renting or buying a house. When we were in military quarters, we did not receive this allowance; it was withheld to pay for the cost of living in those quarters. Thus, we began our civilian life hoping we could make it on Ray's retirement and my small beginning salary. We had an accumulation of U.S. Savings Bonds, which military personnel were encouraged to buy each month, and we dutifully did so for the entire time that Ray was in the Army. Most of these bonds had matured, and, as a result, we were able to make a large part of our down payment on the house by cashing them in.

21 Honeybee Lane, Taylors, SC

We loved this house; it was large and roomy—four bedrooms, two and a half baths, living room, dining room, breakfast room, study, family room, and kitchen. It was on a golf course, except this time the backyard was alongside the course instead of in front of the house, as had been the case with the quarters on Rock Island Arsenal. This house did have some problems; it seemed as if either the furnace or the air conditioner went out every year. However, it was ours, and we could do what we wanted with it, so we did a little remodeling but not much. After all, we were used to making do with what we had!

Leslie was able to go to school with the same friends from fourth through twelfth grades, which was wonderful for her and so different from what I had gone through as a child. She discovered her love of acting and music in middle and high school, performed in several plays in the community and in school, and was active, as were Ray and I, in St. Andrews Presbyterian Church. After she graduated from Wade Hampton High School in 1988, she attended Winthrop University, earning a bachelor's degree in theatre with a teaching certificate. Her first teaching job was at Mt. Airy Junior High School, Mt. Airy, North Carolina, After a year there, she went to J.L. Mann High School in Greenville, South Carolina, to teach, and then to her alma mater, Wade Hampton, where she taught for several years before relocating to the University of South Carolina in Columbia to get her master's degree. Afterwards she taught drama at Lexington High School in Lexington, SC, married Eric Dellinger in January 2004, and resigned in June 2009 when she learned that they would be having a baby in the fall.

Ray explored his options after retirement. He went to real estate school and took a job with a local real estate firm, but after a couple of years he decided the real estate business was not for him. He said, "I got tired of buying people lunch and then never seeing them again." He went back to school, using his G.I. Bill entitlement, with the goal of earning a master's degree in math education. He first took some background courses at Greenville Technical College and then earned his master's at Converse College in Spartanburg, which is an undergraduate women's college but has coed graduate courses. He taught part time a few semesters at North Greenville College where I was employed.

In the meantime I was finding much joy in teaching at a small college and rose to increasingly responsible positions with better salaries. Maybe coming on board as a mature person was helpful. I became chair of the humanities division and really enjoyed my work. Since it was only a two-year school, there were a limited number of English courses offered. I taught first-year composition and British literature, and as I was getting into my tenth year, I began to think I might like to be able to teach more courses, so I started applying for openings.

When an offer came from the academic dean of Gardner-Webb, a four-year college (now a university) in Boiling Springs, NC, it was not easy to leave the place we had lived longer than anywhere else—ten years in one house. Also Ray had his golfing buddies, we had made wonderful friends, and we loved our house. However, I took the plunge, and it was the best decision I ever made. The teaching load at Gardner-Webb was far more interesting with a variety of courses, the faculty members were more diverse, and I advanced to positions of increasing responsibility there as well: Dean of the Graduate School and, finally, Associate Provost for Schools, which enabled me to become the first female to serve on the president of the university's senior staff and put me in charge of the six schools which were at that time part of Gardner-Webb; another associate provost was in charge of the various departments.

Unfortunately, however, we took two years to sell our beautiful house due to a slump in the housing market about the time we put it up for sale--1989. During that period of time I lived in our 22-foot camper in a campground on Moss Lake in Shelby, NC, about twenty minutes from the college. All of my flexibility skills were put to good use during this period. We had moved our camper to this location in order to get it out of our driveway in South Carolina while we were trying to sell our house. The campground was quite nice; it served as a boat dock, had a high chain link fence surrounding it, and the gate was locked at night. There was also a caretaker who lived in a camper on the premises, so I felt quite safe, and Ray and I assumed this was a temporary solution until our house sold in a matter of weeks or months. Of course, that time frame didn't happen!

As we began to realize that I might be living in the camper longer than we expected, Ray fixed up my living arrangements as best he could by building me a porch and making some improvements inside the camper. He stayed in our big, beautiful house with our dog (another poodle, this one named Coco) while waiting for a buyer. Every Monday morning I would leave home with my clothes for the week, drive to campus, teach my classes, drive to the camper, unload my belongings, and settle in for the week. It was a fairly lonely existence: I prepared for classes, read, took walks, watched some TV, and that's about it. On Friday mornings I would pack up, drive to campus, teach my classes, and drive back home for the weekend. My colleagues on campus started referring to me as the "happy camper," although I was far from happy about the situation.

My Residence During the Work Week
from August 1989-May 1991

Since cell phones were still not widely in use and my location would not have allowed me to use one anyway, I would call Ray from a pay phone once a week to see if anyone had come to look at the house. This routine went on for the entire two years until we sold the house, and that was only after I decided we needed to do some redecorating and make some other changes to it. Part of the problem with not being able to sell the house, in addition to the housing slump, was that we had not done much redecorating during the ten years we had lived there. We were used to adjusting to whatever we happened to be living in. We did do a few things, such as transforming a screened-in porch into a walled-in family room, adding a breakfast room and putting down new carpet. However, the kitchen still had 1970s green appliances, the living and dining rooms had busy-looking green and gold wallpaper, the den had dark paneling, and the house had other dated features that we had not bothered to change. After about eighteen months of the house not selling, I contacted a friend who managed a wallpaper shop and who knew something about interior design. With her and her husband's help, we did some renovations, and the house then sold within a few months.

While in the Army we had always had professional moving companies to handle our furniture and other belongings. The one good thing that came out of waiting for two years was that we had time to make this move ourselves with a little paid help from students and friends. Ray bought a used trailer and hooked it to the back of his Blazer; he would bring a load up to our new area at his leisure and put the items in our two rented storage rooms. We also did all of the packing ourselves. When our new home was ready, I hired a couple of football players who were in one of my classes, and they helped Ray move everything in and place it. The one problem with this arrangement was that these two football players were so large they sometimes had a hard time getting a piece of furniture through a doorway while they were carrying it. Ray suggested the next time I need to find two basketball players, who tend to be taller and thinner, although I am hoping there is not a next time!

During the two years we were waiting for our house in Taylors to be sold, we had looked at homes in the area and had also looked at lots for sale. We decided to build in Boiling Springs on a beautiful wooded lot with a creek in front. I had always said I wanted a house with a babbling brook in the front yard. We brought our house plans with us and hired a local builder. We watched our house being built and, because our builder had a dedicated team of his own, construction took only four months. It was a great joy to watch it going up.

Since this was our first experience with building our own house, we made a few mistakes, most of which would have been caught if Ray had been able to be on the building site daily, which he had planned to do since I was at Gardner-Webb all day working. However, it was during this period that his prostate cancer was diagnosed; his surgery took place not long after we moved into our rental apartment. Because of complications, he had limited mobility for most of the time that our house was being built. None of our moves have been free of complications, although this was by far the most serious one. Nevertheless, our house is a well built one, and we have now been in it over twenty years, which is more than twice as long as I have ever lived anywhere.

My first priority, of course, was my work, but I was also interested in at long last being involved in the community. It took a few years before I began to be asked to serve on community boards and committees and to become an active citizen. Perhaps what helped me most of all was deciding to run for the Boiling Springs Town Council. I had spoken to the Council on a street-paving issue one evening in 1998, and as I did, I noticed that all of the members were male— not one female among them, yet 52% of the inhabitants of the town of Boiling Springs at that time were female. That fact convinced me to run for office, so I formed a committee, printed some cards, posted some signs in yards, and pounded the pavement. People kept telling me that I would have a difficult time winning because I had lived in the town only eight years. It helped to have my university colleagues behind me. I won the seat in November 1999, the first woman to serve on that body, and have been re-elected three times. By attending various government and civic meetings, I became acquainted with folks, and, before long, I began to be asked to serve on boards and committees. Public service has been very satisfying for me, and I can see why people want to be involved in that way. However, military life, with its constant moves, does not lend itself to public service very easily.

Our House in Boiling Springs

With the marriage of Leslie and Eric, the military cycle of the family continued: First, my father had served during World War II, then my husband during Vietnam, and, finally, my son-in-law during the Iraq and Afghanistan wars when he was stationed in Kuwait but occasionally had to ride in convoys into Iraq. This was a stressful year for the two of them, as convoys were often hit by IEDs. Ironically, while it was not the best year for Eric, it was Leslie's most successful teaching year; she was selected as the school district's teacher of the year and became nationally certified.

Eric, Luke, and Leslie, December 2012

Eric and Leslie had several separations after their wedding due to Eric's Army orders—the year in Kuwait, temporary duty assignments, and so forth—typical of military life. He decided to retire in 2007 after 20 years, and they have lived as civilians in Lexington, SC, since his retirement from the Army. I wonder if my grandson, 4-year-old Luke, will follow the family tradition and join the military or go another route. I hope to be around to see what he decides to do. He already seems to be flexible and able to adjust to different situations, prime pre-requisites for the military life, not that I am advocating his being in the service, but I would not be disappointed either.

Our 50th Wedding Anniversary, December 29, 2008

Ray and I have now been married over fifty years and were honored in 2008 with a lovely 50th wedding anniversary dinner given by Eric and Leslie. They prepared a special video showcasing our travels and events over the years, which we were able to share with over eighty family members and friends. We have, like most other couples, had plenty of difficulties to deal with, but we have survived them. Would the fifty plus years have been a bit easier without all of the moves? Probably yes, but would those years have been as exciting? Probably not.

CHAPTER FOURTEEN

Comparing Military and Civilian Life

After more than thirty years of military life and and more than thirty years of civilian life, I think I have a strong basis on which to make a comparison. First of all, a person who has been associated with the American military thinks differently from a lifelong civilian. This fact was made clear to me recently while I was working a crossword puzzle. One of its clues was "dogtag datum"— five letters, the last two being "er." I immediately thought of the "dogtags" a military person wears, those small metallic plates on a chain around the neck that have punched into them the person's name, blood type, religious affiliation, and social security number. (The dogtags used to also include a separate serial number which was different from the social security one.) I could not figure out how any of those pieces of information fit into the five spaces. Finally, after working on other parts of the puzzle and returning to this clue, it dawned on me:

The clue referred to *real* dogtags, the ones dogs wear, and the answer was "owner."

Another example is the way we military folks think of machinery such as tanks, guns, trucks, and so forth. We see them as being there for our protection, but a European woman told me that these things scared her because they brought up unpleasant memories from World War II when her homeland was under occupation by another country's military. The American military mind set is definitely different from that of a civilian's.

There are many areas that I could use in making further comparisons, but I will concentrate on four major ones: schools, jobs, churches, and travel. As I wrote earlier, transferring to a new school was always traumatic, more so if the school was in a civilian town or city where the other children had known each other most or all of their lives. In the 40s and 50s schools had their own curricula, so sometimes I would be ahead of the class and sometimes behind. When we joined my dad in Panama in 1947, it was December and the middle of the 5th grade for me. I had always been an A, B student, but I was so far behind the Canal Zone school system that I began making Cs and Ds. I did get caught up but not before I suffered some mental anguish and put in a lot of hard work. Of course, walking into a classroom as a shy 10-year-old, without knowing another person in the room, does not help. There were other military brats as well as Canal Zone civilian children, but, as usual, I felt like the outsider. Obviously, children who have grown up in one community all of their lives may feel like an outsider from feelings of inadequacy in other ways, but it is not because they don't know other children in their classes. I have no idea how many elementary schools I attended, but it had to have been at least six, maybe even more, considering how much we moved. And then, of course, there were those five different high schools.

Trying to get a job back in the 50s, 60s, and 70s was difficult for a military spouse because any potential employer knew that I would not be around more than two to three years and less during the Vietnam War era. After my first experience in Lawton, OK, when I was hired to teach right before Ray received his orders for Panama, I managed to get jobs teaching only part time as I have explained earlier. Also, there is not much networking for the spouse of a military person, since every move involves meeting new people at the next post and town or city. Networking did exist for the military person, especially if that person knew someone in the assignment office in D.C. or if that person were a graduate of a military school, such as West Point. Otherwise, jobs were by chance or luck of the draw. There were only two assignments that Ray asked for and got: Vietnam, for the second time to get out of his ROTC teaching assignment at the University of Southern Mississippi, and Germany. The rest of the assignments were complete surprises but enjoyable ones for the most part, except for Ray's first tour to Vietnam. Basically, we had very little control over the jobs he would have as an Army officer or that I could have as an Army spouse.

Attending church had been an on-again, off-again kind of thing as I was growing up. My parents had both been raised in church-going families but had gotten out of the habit after marriage and with all of the moves. However, as we three children began to grow, they made a concentrated effort to become more active by attending Sunday services and taking us. In fact, during our stint at Fort Hood, TX, our family was the largest one in church one Sunday for which we received a Bible. My parents did not teach Sunday School, though, or become active in church life. However, it was not as easy to do so in military chapels because in those days there were only three services: Protestant, Catholic, and Jewish. The minister assigned to hold Protestant services on a post could be any denomination: Baptist, Methodist, Presbyterian, or whatever. The services were fairly formulaic, other than the sermons, which depended on the particular leanings of the minister. Today Army chaplains offer more diversity, to include Islamic, Lutheran, Episcopalian, and Latter Day Saints services.

After Ray and I married, we attended sporadically until Leslie came along, when we began attending regularly. It was a bit difficult to feel too close to a church congregation when almost everyone who attended was there for just two or three years. However, after Ray's retirement from the Army, we became active in the churches of both communities in which we have lived as civilians: St. Andrews Presbyterian in Taylors, SC, and Shelby Presbyterian in Shelby, NC. Because the church in Taylors had recently been formed, it was easier to feel at home there since all of us were new to the church. However, in Shelby, it took several years before I no longer felt like an outsider. So many members of the congregation have known each other for years or all of their lives; their children have grown up in the church, and for some families more than two generations have been members. Of course, like all churches, this one welcomed us, but I am still learning about family relationships.

As for travel, we have done quite a bit of it since Ray's retirement and especially after I retired from Gardner-Webb, making us both free to go whenever we pleased. As civilians, we have had some wonderful trips, many of them as part of the Road Scholar (formerly Elderhostel) program. Through that program we have been to Seattle; New Orleans; St. Augustine; Branson; Georgia's islands; Natural Bridge, VA; and other places in the States, as well as Scandinavia and Southeast Asia overseas. The latter included visits to four countries: Thailand, Laos, Cambodia, and Vietnam. We discovered Vietnam to be a dynamic, developing country, so different from when Ray was there during the war, which the Vietnamese refer to as the American War. We found the people of Southeast Asia to be friendly and gentile.

The Vietnamese often greeted us with their index and middle fingers forming a V sign. We never quite figured out if they were giving a peace or a victory sign; maybe they were doing both! While in the southern part of the country, we traveled to the area in which Ray was stationed during his first tour—Long An Province, south of Saigon (now Ho Chi Minh City). Where there used to be jungle and dirt roads, there are now a city and paved highways. After the trip Ray said he would never have recognized it if the Vietnamese guide had not told him where we were. He has fond memories of many of the South Vietnamese military and civilians that he worked with during his second tour and wonders at times what became of them after the war.

During our visit to Hanoi, we heard a lecture given by Huu Ngoc, a famous Vietnamese writer and educator. In seventy-five minutes he gave us three thousand years of Vietnamese history and kept our group spellbound. I bought his book, *Wandering Through Vietnamese Culture*, which I read after I returned home. The book, published in 2004, is a compilation of the author's "Traditional Miscellany" columns written for *Viet Nam News* during a ten-year span. It consists of vignettes of Vietnamese life and is a fascinating read, in spite of its one thousand ninety-five pages, longer than *Gone With the Wind*. As a side note, Huu Ngoc writes in his book that the Vietnamese language contains only words of one syllable; that is why place names that we make into one word are two words for them. Thus, the Vietnamese write Ha Noi instead of Hanoi, Sai Gon instead of Saigon, and Viet Nam instead of Vietnam.

Before I retired from Gardner-Webb, I had the opportunity to travel with a university group of faculty, staff, and students to Kenya and Tanzania for two weeks, and an English department colleague and I led a group of adults and students on a ten-day trip to England. All of the above trips have been fun and interesting and educational; however, just visiting a country versus living in one is vastly different. One does not learn much about a country, its people and their customs by a visit, even of a couple of weeks. And a cruise to a country, such as the one we took to Scandinavia or our adventure cruise in Costa Rica, is like fast forwarding a DVD: One gets a glimpse of the content but misses the real story. Obviously, living in a country for a few years as one does in the military is so much more desirable in learning about the culture and the people. The little ability I have in speaking Spanish and German came about through living in Spanish- and German-speaking countries. My limited understanding of French and Italian is primarily a result of not having lived in any of the countries in which those languages are spoken, but only having visited them and having picked up a few words and phrases from a book.

Overall, even with the frustrations and challenges that come with military life, it can be a very enriching experience in many different ways.

CHAPTER FIFTEEN

Afterthoughts

After having lived in both worlds, what conclusions can I draw? If I had my life to live over, would I want to go through the trials and tribulations of a military life again? To answer the last question first, I give a resounding yes. Although I am becoming more set in my ways as I get older, I can still adapt to almost any situation I face. I would not take anything for most of the experiences I had while a daughter and a wife of military men, although I hasten to add that I prefer the latter to the former, primarily because of the difference in salary, housing accommodations, and duties between a non-commissioned officer, such as my dad, and a commissioned officer, such as my husband. I am fully aware that many of the problems my family faced as I was growing up, and even those that Ray and I faced, were the direct result of decisions that could have been made differently if we had only known what lay in store for us. On the other hand, the very nature of military life brings about situations that require families to make decisions that they would not otherwise have to worry about.

Along with the rootlessness of military life, I had the opportunity to travel and to live in different countries and states. I also learned how to make a home out of whatever type of residence we might find ourselves in, from a small apartment or mobile home to a huge set of Army quarters which I dare not paint or carpet or leave open holes in walls where I had hung pictures. Each move meant a different supervisor for Ray and learning to adjust to what that person required; it also meant a new commanding officer's wife and adjusting to her wishes for the other wives in terms of social life. I already knew of the problem with changing schools from my own childhood, but I learned about the importance of being able to adjust all over again from my daughter, although she had to change elementary schools only three times because Ray retired from the military after she had completed the third grade. We have just the one child; I often wondered how families with five, six, and seven children were able to manage in the military, but they did and continue to do so. We all learned to cherish old friends and to keep in communication with them but to meet new ones quickly as well.

There was a comfort in knowing that each military post to which Ray was assigned had the same types of facilities: a post exchange, a commissary, a Class VI store (where the military go to buy their alcohol at reduced prices), a library, a hospital or clinic (depending on the size of the installation), an officers' club with a swimming pool and golf course, an NCO club, living quarters (although rarely enough for all of the married personnel assigned), and so forth. In addition, there was always the chance of running into people Ray had been assigned with previously.

Finally, a down side to living the military life meant seeing our extended families only rarely and not always being able to attend funerals and weddings. Both Ray's grandmother and brother died while we were in Germany, and he could not get to the funerals because of his work situation and the length of time it would take to get to Kentucky for his grandmother and to Florida for his brother. I did not really get to know and be friends with my first cousins until after Ray had retired, our children were grown, and all of us were free enough to be able to attend family reunions, weddings, and funerals.

While civilian life certainly has its hassles and concerns, at least a person can have roots. As civilians for the last thirty plus years, we have owned two houses and have been able to remodel, paint, wallpaper, change carpet, and make any kinds of adjustments we want to our own home. Clerks at the bank, the grocery store, the drugstore, the post office, the library, and so forth know us and trust us. We now have friends that we have known for thirty years or more who live in the same area in which we first met them and plan to stay where they are until they cannot do so any longer, as do we. In other words, we now have a network on which we can rely for information about which plumber or electrician to call or anything else. We have a home church where people know us. Our daughter was able to go to one middle school and one high school and made lots of friends, many of whom she still communicates with. Of course, email, Facebook, Skype, and cell phones make communication much easier now than decades earlier when Ray and I had to rely on regular mail and tape recorders. All of these advantages bring a feeling of comfort and belongingness in the community.

When I am asked now where I am from, I have an answer. I reply that I am from the town in which I live, Boiling Springs, even though someone who knows me well might say, "She's not really from here; she's been here only twenty-some years." Because Ray was born, grew up, and attended school in one town before he went off to college and then entered the Army, he would answer that question by saying "Winchester, KY." He has roots, and I am beginning to grow them. As for the question of where I want to be buried, I still have no idea, but I know it's an issue I need to be thinking seriously about and making a decision.

Living the military life was a valuable experience that cost me in many ways, but it gave me so much more than it took from me.

ACKNOWLEDGMENTS

Gratitude and thanks go to several of my friends and family members who read this book in its various stages and offered suggestions. Joyce Brown, who was in the doctoral program with me at Southern Mississippi and was also a colleague in the English department at Gardner-Webb University, read it in first draft and in a later draft and was instrumental in helping me make stronger word choices and better placement of paragraphs. Kathryn Hamrick, who took time out from her own writing project of editing and publishing her newspaper columns, also read the document twice and made valuable suggestions. Others who read it and offered helpful advice were Barbara Blackburn, an avid reader and friend, and Kathleen Boehmig, whom I met at Wildacres at the 2013 Spring Gathering, and who read parts of it.

Most importantly, those who know me best—my husband, Ray; my daughter, Leslie; and my brother, Richard-- read the document with critical eyes, alerting me to some life experiences I had failed to mention as well as pointing out confusing stories or those needing elaboration. I was particularly concerned about embarrassing them with stories of their past, but all three gave me the go-ahead. I am indebted to them for their sage advice.

My son-in-law, Eric, read the final draft with a view toward spotting any military or other misstatements.

I have been working on this story of my life in phases for many years, so I hope I am forgiven if I have failed to mention someone along the way who read it that I have totally forgotten about. Any mistakes in it are due to my poor memory or negligence, not to any of my readers.

Made in United States
North Haven, CT
28 February 2024

49304721R00088